Authentication and Authorization on the Web

Authentication and Authorization on the Web

Nigel Chapman and Jenny Chapman

MacAvon Media

Web Security Topics Series

Authentication and Authorization on the Web

Published by MacAvon Media
Achnaha House, Kilchoan, Acharacle PH36 4LW Scotland (UK)

www.macavonmedia.com

ISBN: 978-0-9567370-5-2

Contents

About This Book

The short books in the *Web Security Topics* series have been designed to provide Web developers with the essential practical information they need to protect their applications against attack in the increasingly hostile world of the modern Internet. Each book focuses on a specific area of interest.

Security has become an issue that no Web developer can afford to ignore. Scarcely a week goes past without news of a break-in occurring at some high-profile Web site. Sometimes the result is just a temporary loss of service, but all too often passwords, personal information and credit card details are stolen. Only the attacks on well-known sites reach the news, but there are countless other unreported attacks on smaller sites which, although not newsworthy, are nevertheless of great importance to the small businesses that own them, to their customers, and to the developers responsible for building and maintaining those sites.

Most books on Web security are aimed not at working developers but at security specialists and professional security consultants. Those books are dedicated to examining the intricacies of particular forms of attack, to the extent that it sometimes seems as though they are manuals for potential attackers. We have therefore written this series of short books to focus specifically on the areas of interest to Web developers. We describe and explain only what developers need to know in order to defend their own applications against attack, leaving more time free for the creation of exciting and useful Web applications.

In this book we are concerned with ensuring that the resources managed by an application are protected so that they can only be manipulated by the users and programs entitled to do so. Conventionally, this is achieved by setting up user accounts protected by passwords and requiring users to log in, so we begin by describing how user accounts can be maintained and how passwords can be kept safe and secure. We go on to consider authentication, which is the process of verifying the identity of a user sending a request. This is usually done by requiring the user to provide their correct password when they log in, and by using cookies to remember their identity and associate it with subsequent requests, although we also consider some alternative arrangements.

It is a relatively simple matter to identify the owner of each resource and assign roles to users. A system of authorization can then be implemented to ensure that each request from a user will only be honoured by the application if their role gives them the necessary privileges to perform the requested operation on the resource identified in the request's URL.

We have developed a simple Web application, using the Express framework, as an example which runs throughout the book. Code extracts from this application are used to illustrate each principle as it is introduced. The application is written in JavaScript, a language which should be familiar to all Web developers. Some of the more advanced JavaScript programming techniques in our examples, and the use of Express and Node.js to create a JavaScript application that runs outside a browser, may perhaps be less familiar. A free short tutorial on these subjects is provided on the series' companion Web site at www.websecuritytopics.info. The code for the examples is also available for free download – visit the companion site for details of how to obtain it.

In order to humanize what can be a dry subject, we have adapted the characters of Abelardo and his beloved Lady Gwendolen, who we found in our collection of obscure older films. Together with their associates, the pair feature in all the books in the *Web Security Topics* series. It seemed appropriate to place these characters in Freedonia, a country that also belongs in the movie archives, and has the advantage of a country TLD, .fd, which is not actually assigned in reality. Where it matters, we have tested examples using .fd domain names on a specially configured local server. Abelardo and friends are expert tiddlywinks players. We may have made up the characters, but the tiddlywinks jargon they sometimes employ is authentic.

This book includes a full glossary of the (non-tiddlywinks) technical terms which are used in the text. The first significant occurrence of each term defined in the glossary is printed in **bold italics**.

The companion Web site for all the books in the *Web Security Topics* series provides further information, useful links and supporting material. Visit the site at www.websecuritytopics.info.

The fact that some examples in this book refer to the code sharing service Github should not be taken as an endorsement of Github's services by the authors or publisher, nor as an endorsement of this text by Github.

Important Disclaimer

The example code in this book is provided solely for the purposes of illustrating some principles and techniques of authentication and authorization. It is not intended for serious use in sensitive applications. Neither the publisher nor the authors shall be liable for any consequence arising from the use of program code in this book for any purpose other than illustration of general principles in the context of learning.

Electronic Formats

This book is published in both print and electronic formats. For full details of the currently available editions, please check the publisher's Web site www.macavonmedia.com or the companion site for the *Web Security Topics* series at www.websecuritytopics.info.

Introduction

The process of *authorization* – deciding whether an application should be allowed to carry out the operation which a request from a particular user or program calls for – depends on, but is separate from, *authentication*, which means determining the identity of the user or program sending that request. It is a pity that the names are so easily confused, because failure to distinguish between the two processes is a potential source of security weaknesses. A user who has been authenticated is usually still subject to some restrictions on the resources they can access.

Resources are the entities that make up the World Wide Web. Each resource is identified by a Uniform Resource Locator, or URL. Resources are retrieved and manipulated in response to HTTP requests sent from clients – usually Web browsers – to servers, which generally pass them on to application code running on the server host. The data comprising most resources manipulated by Web applications is stored in databases, which provide means of creating, retrieving, updating and deleting resources – a set of operations collectively known as CRUD. On the Web, authorization is thus the process of determining whether performing these operations on a resource should be allowed or denied in response to a request from a particular client.

To appreciate how authorization and authentication can be performed by Web applications, you need to understand **HTTP**, the protocol on which the Web is built, so we will provide a brief summary of its operation.

HTTP and Web Applications

The Web is built on the client/server model of distributed systems. The programs that participate in the Web are of two kinds: clients, which send requests for resources, and servers, which listen for incoming requests and return a representation of the requested resource. The most common type of HTTP client is the familiar Web browser, though mobile applications often behave as HTTP clients, usually only sending requests to one particular server. HTTP servers come in many forms, including general-purpose servers such as Apache and Nginx, and specialized servers that implement a single Web application.

HTTP defines the interaction between Web servers and clients, and the format of the messages they exchange. It assumes there is a reliable transport mechanism to carry these messages – in practice TCP/IP is used for this purpose. Messages sent from the client to the server are called *requests*, and those sent back from the server to the client are *responses*. URLs are used in requests from clients to identify resources. The host name in the URL (the part of the URL between the http:// prefix and the first /)identifies the host on which the server to which the request is directed is running. The remainder of the URL (the path) specifies the resource on that host.

The simplest interaction between a Web client and server occurs when a user clicks on a link in a Web page being displayed in their browser. Suppose the link points to the site for Abelardo's Tiddlywinks Club. This link will be an HTML a element, with its href attribute's value set to the URL of the site's home page, which might be http://www.abelardos.com.fd/index.html. When the link is clicked, the user's browser performs a DNS lookup to find the IP address of the host www.abelardos.com.fd and sends a request. This being a simple request to retrieve a resource, the HTTP verb GET is used. The request consists of the *request line*

```
GET /index.html HTTP/1.1
```

followed by some headers containing information about the type of data the browser will accept and some metadata about the request. One significant header repeats the host name. This allows the server to direct the request to the appropriate process when multiple virtual hosts share an IP address.

On receiving such a request, the Web server looks for the resource it identifies. In this case the resource is simply a static file, so the path part of the URL can be treated as a file system path, identifying the file's location within the part of the file system accessible to the Web server. The server sends a response, which normally begins with the status line

```
HTTP/1.1 200 OK
```

indicating that all is well. This is followed by some headers containing similar information to those in the request. The headers are followed by the contents of the file, which constitute the body of a response, so that the browser can display it, possibly after sending some more requests for images and other assets required by the page. HTTP supports an elaborate system of caching to optimize network usage, so requests may sometimes be handled in a slightly different way, but we need not be concerned with this refinement.

Static Web sites, where the content consists entirely of HTML documents stored on disk, can be accessed exclusively by way of simple GET requests. There is usually no need to apply any authorization to the requests, because such sites are generally intended to be accessible to all visitors. Most threats to the security of static sites come from attackers gaining access to the server host, which can allow them to deface the site or to commandeer it to host illicit content. (We describe defences against attacks of this sort in the volume *A Web Developer's Guide to Securing a Server* in this series.) If some pages are confidential, the server need only filter requests that refer to those pages, using a simple method described in the chapter on *Authentication*.

Authorization is a more interesting problem in dynamically generated Web sites. In such sites, users are often able to create and update their own resources and determine who should be allowed to see them. Web browsers send POST and PUT requests, with data in their bodies, and this data is processed by server-side code, which may combine it with data stored in a database to generate responses.

Most contemporary Web applications of any complexity are built using one of the many Web application development frameworks available for the purpose. Frameworks deal with the repetitive tasks that are part of every application, only calling code written by the developer to perform the computation that is specific to a particular application. Currently popular frameworks include Rails and Sinatra, which are written in Ruby; Django and Pyramid, in Python; CodeIgniter, Symfony and Kohana in PHP; Catalyst in Perl; and countless others. In this book, we shall use *Express*, a JavaScript framework built on top of *Node.js*, for our examples.

All these frameworks loosely follow the *Model-View-Controller (MVC)* pattern. An application is logically divided into three separate types of module, each of which deals with one aspect of the task of responding to incoming requests. *Models* access and modify data, which is usually stored in a database. *Views* present data, that is, they render it so that users can perceive it. In a Web application, views generate HTML to be sent in the body of HTTP responses. *Controllers* coordinate everything. The way most Web frameworks are arranged, each controller consists of a collection of methods or functions that invoke model operations to retrieve or alter some data and then render a view, usually by interpolating data into a template. A routing module that is part of the framework examines the URL path in each incoming request, and on the basis of rules defined by the developer, passes control to a controller method, making the data in the request available to the called method. (Some software pattern zealots insist that this pattern isn't "really" MVC, but it is how the name is normally used in Web development.)

In a Web application that uses an MVC framework, the interaction between the client and the application is a little more complicated than the simple interaction we described above. Although frameworks may incorporate an HTTP server to handle requests and send responses directly, a general-purpose Web server, such as Apache, is often used to listen for all incoming requests on an IP address, and pass on to the Web application any requests which are directed to the appropriate host name, using reverse proxying or some other mechanism. The application returns its responses by the same method, and the server sends them on to the client. The server merely acts as an intermediary in such an arrangement, so we need not be concerned with its role in the interaction.

The architecture of Web applications built in this way means that actions can only be invoked by HTTP requests. Nothing else can invoke a controller method, and so nothing else can cause a model to retrieve or change data. While this can be a source of frustration to the developer, it has the important consequence that authorization can be performed in a single place, between the routing and the controller.

Each framework provides its own way of defining routes and specifying code to be executed before controller methods are called, but they are all roughly similar. In Express, a server object is created and conventionally assigned to a variable called app. Routing is specified by calling methods through this object. The routing methods (get, post, put, del) are named after the HTTP verbs and there is also a method all, which is used to specify routing for URLs that does not depend on the HTTP verb.

For example, suppose a controller module called userController exported methods called show, create and update, among others, which retrieved, created and updated user profiles in some application. Conventionally, we would route the URL /user to one of these methods, depending on the HTTP verb in the request: GET requests should call the show method, POST requests call the create method and PUT requests call the update method. This could be achieved using the following routes:

```
app.get('/user', userController.show);
app.post('/user', userController.create);
app.put('/user', userController.update);
```

If any user of the application was allowed to see any other user's profile data, no authorization would need to be applied to GET requests. If users can create their own accounts, no authorization can be applied to POST requests. However, updating a profile is something that should only be permitted to its owner. Express allows the developer to pass additional callbacks to the routing methods, which will be called before control is passed to the controller method. These callbacks are referred to as *route middleware*. Authorization is one of the most useful applications of route middleware. The middleware stands between the incoming request and the controller, exactly as we require.

If we could define a function restrictToAuthenticated, which ensured that a request was being sent by a legitimate user of the application and retrieved the user profile for that user, it could be used as middleware on the route for PUT requests, like this:

```
app.put('/user', restrictToAuthenticated,
                 userController.update);
```

This arrangement is nice and neat but relies on the application being able to associate incoming requests with users. To be more precise, it relies on being able to associate incoming requests with some data stored by the application to serve as an identifier for some entity, such as a human user or a program that has been granted permission to make calls to the application. The means of association must not be vulnerable to deception, that is, it must not be possible for the application to be misled by requests which claim to be coming from some legitimate entity but in fact are not.

The first prerequisite for being able to make this association is the existence of data which can be used to identify entities that may legitimately send requests. Unless it allows all visitors free access to all the resources it manages, a Web application needs to maintain records that represent users and programs which might legitimately send requests that cause restricted operations to be performed on resources. In the case of human users, these records are kept in the accounts which they must create in order to access the application. User accounts also have other purposes, providing a place to collect together all sorts of information about each user, but for the purposes of security their main function is just to provide a record of a user's identity and a way to confirm it. Web applications therefore need to provide a means for people to create accounts, and may need some way of allowing other programs to be registered before they can be permitted to access data.

The process of confirming identity is **authentication**. Because programs lack any intelligence or real knowledge, authentication by software is not simple. The conventional formula concerning methods of authentication states that you can prove your identity using one or more of "something you are, something you have and something you know". In small communities, most authentication is based on physical appearance – people recognize each other because they know what they look like. Where computer programs are doing the authentication, though, some representation of a person's physical characteristics that can be digitized and processed algorithmically is needed, hence the use of biometric data, such as fingerprints and retinal scans, in high-security systems.

In larger organizations, ID cards are often used as a means of identifying people, by virtue of something they have. An ID card only serves as authentication if there is reason to believe that the person showing the card came by it legitimately. Often, it is necessary to be able to demonstrate that the "something you have" is indeed yours. For instance, staff ID cards usually bear a photograph of the holder – in other words, they ultimately rely on authentication by appearance.

The third way of identifying yourself is by some shared secret knowledge. Passwords and secret handshakes have been used in this way for centuries, by armies and clandestine organizations, for example. Although passwords are seldom used as a means of getting in to office buildings or university departments, they are almost ubiquitous as a means of getting access to computer systems. The characteristic flaw in schemes based on shared secret knowledge is precisely that it is necessary to share the knowledge between the entity being authenticated and the entity doing the authentication, and it is necessary to do so secretly. Anybody who knows a password can provide it as a means of authentication, no matter whether they came by the password legitimately or otherwise.

For authentication to be possible, the person or system to whom you need to identify yourself must know about the thing you are, have or know. Arranging this in advance with a remote Web application is difficult, except in the case of "something you know". Although high-security applications such as online banking have mechanisms for checking something you have – usually a device for generating unique tokens – the overhead of setting up such a scheme is not usually considered worthwhile for more commonplace Web applications. The easiest option – sharing knowledge of some secret – is the most common. In a typical Web application, a user chooses a password when they sign up, and must provide it before they are allowed to perform restricted operations on resources.

Performing authentication over HTTP presents additional difficulties, because HTTP is a stateless protocol. This means that once the server has sent a response, it discards all information about the request it has just been dealing with. A user cannot provide their password once and then be recognized as the source of subsequent requests unless their browser sends information in the request that the Web application can match against some persistent data which it maintains for the purpose. This is usually done by way of HTTP cookies, although other mechanisms may be used, as we shall describe in the chapter on *Authentication*.

The majority of Web applications currently rely on a combination of passwords and cookies. When a user creates an account on a site, he makes up a password, which he keeps secret. When he signs in to the application, he must provide the password to prove that he is who he claims to be. If he is unable to do so, he will only be permitted access to any resources managed by the application which are public, that is, accessible to anybody.

If information can be associated with user accounts to indicate which resources the account's owner can access, and what they can do with them, authentication provides the basis of a mechanism for enforcing the restrictions that a Web application typically imposes. It isn't usually practical to record the permissions applicable to each user for each individual resource, so users are often assigned roles, such as site administrator, user with a standard account, user with a premium account, and so on, and the permissions are applied to the role. In simple cases, the permissions can be incorporated in the application code. For more complex situations, a declarative means of defining permissions for each user or role is preferable, as it offers more flexibility.

Authorization is needed by operating systems as well as Web applications. In this more mature field, sophisticated methods have been developed for controlling processes' access to resources. The methods commonly employed by Web applications are based on these earlier ideas, although at present the fine level of control offered by some of the more advanced operating system facilities is not usually required.

Databases

The data that constitutes user accounts must be maintained permanently, and so must the other data manipulated by almost all Web applications. This means that the application must communicate with a database. The way applications and databases interact is not specific to authentication and authorization, but it is essential to them. We must therefore devote the rest of this chapter to a digression on the subject of databases, before we can begin our detailed description of authentication and authorization.

For many years, the most popular database systems have been based on the *relational model* of data, in which data is organized as a set of tables, each row of which represents a single entity, while the columns, or fields, are the attributes shared by all the entities in the table. This apparently simple arrangement is extremely powerful, and amenable to efficient programming, but it maps poorly onto the concepts of object-oriented programs. Recently, this mismatch, together with concerns about the applicability of the relational model to the storage of the immense sets of data that are being generated by some modern applications, has led to an interest in alternative types of database, collectively referred to as **NoSQL databases**. In some ways, NoSQL databases provide a better fit for applications written in JavaScript, but we prefer to use a traditional relational database in our examples, as it will be more familiar to most readers and incorporates well-established methods of representing data and the relationships within it.

Broadly speaking, there are two ways of interacting with a relational database system from within a program written in an object-oriented language. *Object-Relational Mapping (ORM)* is a way of allowing the tables in the database to be manipulated as if they were classes, with the rows being objects. The flat, tabular structure of the database is hidden from the program, which can be written almost as if the values in the database were programming language objects with the ability to persist beyond the end of the program's execution. Alternatively, a module can be used that embeds the data manipulation and query operations of the SQL language in the programming language. This lower-level approach is sometimes preferred because relational databases do not map entirely comfortably on to objects.

At the time of writing, there is no mature ORM for Node.js comparable to Active Record in Ruby on Rails or the ORM built in to Django, although several promising systems are in development. We won't use a full ORM, therefore, but instead we will store our objects using a simple module for persistent data that we have built on top of the **Node-DBI** module, a "database-agnostic" driver which provides a single API for several different database systems. This allows us to expose the actual database operations when doing so makes it clearer where security vulnerabilities may lie. In effect, we are creating our own little ORM between the tables in the database and JavaScript objects in our program. Such an abstraction of one or more database tables as a set of objects is often called a *model*.

The details of the implementation of our `persistent_objects` module are of little relevance. If you want to know how the module works, visit www.websecuritytopics.info to find out how to download the source. The module exports several methods, including `save`, `count` and `destroy`, and several methods for retrieving one or more records from the database and creating objects from them. All these methods operate asynchronously, because the underlying database drivers are asynchronous. Therefore, they must all take a callback as an argument instead of returning values.

Listing 1 is a simple module showing how persistent objects are created and used. Our code is organized using the module system provided by Node.js. Any module used to implement persistent objects must take an instance of a `DBWrapper` object, created by Node-DBI as a parameter, and this object must also be made available through a property called `db`. We are not primarily concerned with building an ORM, so we have taken a somewhat lazy approach, and require any object that needs to be stored in the database to have a `table` property giving the name of the database table in which values are to be stored, and a property called `persistentProperties`, which holds the names of the object's properties to be mapped to columns in the table. You can see these declarations on lines 12–25.

Our example models "Things", which have several legs and a distinctive colour. Things can be created by passing an object to the `Thing` constructor, with fields for these two attributes. The constructor declared in lines 4–10 is passed to the function exported by our `persistent_object` module when we require it on line 27. You can think of the module as a factory for making persistent objects out of ordinary objects, so passing it the `Thing` constructor gives back a `persistentThing`, which has the methods necessary for saving Things to the database and retrieving them from it.

The `persistentThing.save` method takes three optional arguments: first a function that may perform some validation, second a message to

Listing 1

```
 1  module.exports = function(db) {
 2
 3    // Constructor
 4    var Thing = function(options) {
 5      if (options) {
 6        this._numberOfLegs = options.numberOfLegs;
 7        this._colour = options.colour;
 8            this._isNew = true;
 9      }
10    };
11
12    // Persistence rubric
13    Thing.persistentProperties = ['_numberOfLegs', '_colour'];
14
15    Object.defineProperty(Thing, 'db', {
16      get: function(){
17        return db;
18      }
19    });
20
21    Object.defineProperty(Thing, 'table', {
22      get: function(){
23        return 'things';
24      }
25    });
26
27    var persistentThing = require('../lib/persistent_objects')
(Thing);
28
29    // Persistence methods
30      Thing.prototype.save = persistentThing.save(
31      function(t) {
32        return t.colour != '' && t.numberOfLegs >= 1;
33      },
34      'Invalid data'
35    );
36
```

```
37  Thing.destroy = persistentThing.destroy('id');
38
39  Thing.count = persistentThing.count;
40
41  // Standard properties
42  Object.defineProperty(Thing.prototype, 'id', {
43   get: function(){
44    return this._id;
45   }
46  });
47
48  Object.defineProperty(Thing.prototype, 'updatedAt', {
49   get: function(){
50    return this._updatedAt;
51   }
52  });
53
54  Object.defineProperty(Thing.prototype, 'createdAt', {
55   get: function(){
56    return this._createdAt;
57   }
58  });
59
60    Thing.prototype.isNew = function() {
61      return this._isNew;
62    };
63
64  // Data properties
65  Object.defineProperty(Thing.prototype, 'numberOfLegs', {
66   get: function(){
67    return this._numberOfLegs;
68   },
69   set: function(n) {
70    this._numberOfLegs = n;
71   }
72  });
73
```

```
74   Object.defineProperty(Thing.prototype, 'colour', {
75     get: function(){
76       return this._colour;
77     },
78     set: function(c) {
79       this._colour = c;
80     }
81   });
82
83   // Finders
84   Thing.findById = function(i, callback) {
85     persistentThing.findOneObject('id = ?', [i], callback);
86   };
87
88   Thing.findByColour = function(c, callback) {
89     persistentThing.findManyObjects('colour = ?', [c], callback);
90   };
91
92   Thing.findByMinimumNumberOfLegs = function(n, callback) {
93     persistentThing.findManyObjects('number_of_legs >= ?', [n],
callback);
94   };
95
96   return Thing;
97 }
```

be used if the validation fails, and third a callback to be applied after the save operation. The arguments are optional. In our example, the third is omitted. The value returned by the call of persistentThing.save on lines 30–35 is assigned to be the actual save method for Thing objects. Since the saving will be performed asynchronously, this method takes a callback as its argument.

We can count the number of Things in the database and delete a Thing with a particular id, using the methods for that purpose belonging to the persistentThing object. We simply assign them as methods of the Thing object, on lines 37–39.

Following a convention adapted from Active Record, we generate unique id values for each object when it is first saved. We also apply time stamps to every object to record the time it was first saved and the time of any subsequent updates. Any object that uses the persistent_objects module should define the standard properties on lines 42–58 to provide access to the values of the id and time stamps. Note that there are no setter functions, because it does not make sense for these values to be changed. We used a flag called _isNew to record whether the object has ever been saved. Although this is primarily for internal purposes, we provide another property for getting its value (lines 60–62).

The values transferred to and from the database are held in "private" properties, whose names begin with an _ character. (JavaScript doesn't support data hiding directly, so these properties are not really private, but the convention is a helpful one. It is possible to implement modules in a more elaborate way that does allow for data hiding, but doing so would obscure the examples, so we prefer to rely on convention in this book.) On lines 65–81 we define a pair of data properties that make them visible. In this example, these are effectively redundant, but in general using this convention allows us to make some of the stored values read-only, or to perform some computation before saving or after retrieving them. We will show some examples of properties of this sort in later chapters.

A Thing object can be retrieved by way of the method findById, defined on lines 84–86, using the unique id value assigned to it when it is first saved. We have also used the finder methods to provide illustrative methods for finding all the Things of a certain colour or possessed of at least a specified number of legs. As you can see, these make use of two methods from the persistent_objects module, findOneObject and findManyObjects. The only tricky aspect of these (besides their being asynchronous) is the form of the arguments used for specifying the records to be retrieved from the database. The first is a string that has the form of the where part of a prepared SQL select statement. That is, it includes ? characters which act as placeholders for the values that determine which records will be retrieved. The second argument is an array of values to be used to replace these placeholders. Thus,

```
Thing.findByMinimumNumberOfLegs = function(7, callback);
```

will call

```
persistentThing.findManyObjects('number_of_legs >= ?', [7],
callback);
```

and the first two arguments will be interpolated into the SQL query

```
select * from things where number_of_legs >= 7;
```

This may seem a roundabout way of constructing the query, but using prepared statements prevents **SQL injection**, one of the most effective forms of attack against Web applications, which is described in full in the book *Web Application Attacks and Defences* in this series.

When we consider the storage of user accounts and the resources managed by a Web application in the following chapters, we will use the technique described here to map the objects manipulated by the application to records in a relational database. We will therefore suppress the common rubric and standard methods in subsequent listings.

User Accounts

Restricting certain operations to authorized users is a fundamental strategy in securing systems and applications. To do this, some means of authentication is required. Once a user's identity has been authenticated, it becomes possible to allow them to perform the operations they are authorized to carry out, and to prevent them from executing any unauthorized actions. However, before we can begin to think about how to restrict operations on a Web site in this way, we need some way of recording who is eligible to use the site. That is, we need some mechanism for creating and managing user accounts.

User accounts are employed in many different types of application. For example, if a Web application provides services that must be paid for, it is necessary to restrict access to those services to just those users who have paid. This is usually done by allowing people to "sign up" and create an account, and by requiring them to provide a valid account name and matching password each time they wish to use the service.

In a similar way, e-commerce sites which trade in physical goods maintain a record of each customer's purchases and other data associated with them by requiring users to create accounts. This also has benefits for the customer, as by signing in to their own account each user is able to monitor their own purchases, make repeat orders, keep lists of favourite items, wish lists, and so on. If an e-commerce site deals in digital goods – such as software, digital audio, video, or e-books – it can keep track of which files each customer is eligible to download by requiring customers to create user accounts.

In other types of application it is common to require users to create an account and log in before they can update content, for instance by posting comments to a blog or uploading images to a photo sharing site. This also allows the site's administrators to impose resource restrictions and to exert some control over users' behaviour – by banning users who post inappropriate content, for example.

Having a unique account gives each user an identity, which makes it possible for users to recognize each other and perhaps rate other users' contributions. User accounts are therefore central to social networking sites, because they provide a means of associating each user and their actions with a profile containing information about them (a feature which is not only exploited by the users themselves). At the same time, the requirement to sign in to an account restricts access to the data associated with that account, so that only the authorized user can alter or add to it.

Not all Web applications require user accounts. It is possible to implement an e-commerce site without them, for example, but in most cases the site can provide additional benefits to its users if it is able to recognize them. Many e-commerce sites do sell goods online without requiring the customer to create an account or log in, but if there is no user account associated with a customer it is not possible to remember their delivery address for the future, keep track of their purchase history, allow them to specify which categories of product they are most interested in, and so on. User accounts provide extra convenience for repeat customers by removing the need to enter the same information each time they make a purchase.

In the case of digital goods, the fact that user accounts enable the application to record which files each user is entitled to download also means that the customer can obtain a new copy if the file is updated or they destroy their existing copy. It is possible to provide a downloads service without accounts, but in that case the only way of controlling access to downloads is by using special URLs that only permit a file to be downloaded once, which provides an inferior service to users.

As well as allowing users to create accounts and log in, most Web applications must provide privileged access for administrators – the people in charge of setting up and maintaining the application. Administrators can perform operations which alter the contents of any pages displayed by the application, and they can read any data stored in its database, so it is essential to ensure that unauthorized persons or programs are not able to gain administrator access. One way of controlling this is by creating a special class of user accounts for administrators, which grant extra privileges. Alternatively, administrator access can be controlled by a separate mechanism from the one used for less privileged users.

User accounts are more than just a way of providing end users with extra facilities and convenience. They are a fundamental security mechanism, providing a basis for preventing users from performing operations they are not authorized to carry out on resources managed by a Web application, and a means of excluding unauthorized visitors from access to all or part of a Web site.

In this chapter we describe the creation and maintenance of user accounts, paying particular attention to the secure storage of passwords. The way in which a user may log in to an application, and ways of restricting access to some operations to administrative users, will be described in the following chapters. For now, it is only necessary to accept that once a user has logged in, a mechanism can be provided for associating their user account with each HTTP request sent by their browser.

Passwords

The main purpose of user accounts is to associate each individual user with the requests that they make, so it's necessary to ensure that only the person who created an account can use it. The most common way of achieving this is by use of a *shared secret* – a value known only to the owner of the account, and stored by the application as part of the account data. The practical difficulties of using *public key certificates* (see the *Notes on Cryptography* at the end of this book) for this purpose are generally considered insuperable, so in most cases the shared secret takes the form of a password or pass phrase.

It is likely that you will have had to choose a password countless times when signing up for Web services of various kinds. You will probably also have had to set a password for controlling your access to a computer. No doubt you have been advised to choose long passwords containing a mixture of upper-case and lower-case letters, digits and punctuation symbols, so that the password is hard to guess or discover by trying words from a dictionary or list of names. The advice is excellent, but the hardness of a password is actually determined by which methods attackers use when trying to discover it. It isn't really an absolute property. Suppose, for example, that because they knew that users are advised to use long passwords, and also knew that most systems enforce a minimum length for passwords, hackers decided there was no longer any point trying to log in to a system by guessing a password with fewer than six characters. In those circumstances, a password with only two characters would be one of the safest you could choose, because no guessing attempt would ever look for or find it. This example is strictly for illustration only. It really is an excellent idea to use longer passwords but, as this example shows, the security of any particular password can only be judged relative to the strategy being used to guess it.

This observation leads to some paradoxes. For instance, consider a pure *brute force attack*, in which every combination of some set of symbols is generated systematically and tried as a password. (This isn't a very practical sort of attack, unless it can be launched by a large collection of machines working cooperatively.) If the set of symbols that the attackers are using consists only of letters, any password containing a digit will be secure. But if the set consists of letters and digits, the probability of any combination being tried is exactly the same. In other words, using a digit in your password makes it secure if no brute-force hacker is looking for digits, but if they are looking for them it makes no difference whether you include a digit in your password or not. The order in which combinations are tried would make a difference to how long it took to reach a particular password, but this is unpredictable, especially if the attempts are being made in parallel.

However, brute force attacks are only part of the story. We know something about the strategies that attackers adopt from looking at logs recording break-in attempts. These attempts take two forms.

Online attacks are those in which somebody is simply visiting the sign-in page, or using a program to send requests to it, in an attempt to log in to a system or Web application to which they do not have legitimate access. In this type of attack they usually just try the entries from a database of common passwords. *Phishing* sites are often used to "harvest" passwords for this purpose. Sometimes, a successful attack against a large site has enabled the attackers to steal its password database. From time to time, copies of illicit password lists are obtained by legitimate security researchers, so we know that, for example, 123456, password1 and qwerty feature near the top of such lists, and are therefore not sensible choices for a password. We also know that attempts are often made to log in without any password, so leaving the password blank is not a good idea. Where a site requires a user name, the name chosen should not also be used as the password, as automated login attempts often use the same value for both. Similarly, if an email address is used to sign in, no part of it should also be used as the password.

Many systems and applications set a default password when they are installed. Databases listing all the default passwords for almost every system that does this are freely available. Research indicates that many administrators never bother to change the default password, so the hacker's common ploy of trying the default password is successful all too often. You should always set your own password as soon as you have completed the installation of any system that sets a default. If you are creating a package for other people to install which will be accessed over the Internet, and it needs an administrator's password, make sure that your system will not work until a password has been set explicitly. Don't set a default or allow the system to be used without a password. If you are a system administrator who is responsible for one or more routers, don't forget to change their passwords from the factory default. Being able to log in to a router offers intruders fruitful opportunities for further attacks.

Online attacks rarely provide an opportunity for extensive password-cracking campaigns. It is common for applications and systems to make the authentication process deliberately slow, or to temporarily deny access to IP addresses from which more than a few unsuccessful login attempts have been made, thereby preventing anybody from making a large number of attempts in a feasible time. However, if the attackers have managed to obtain the file or database in which the encrypted passwords are stored, they will be able to launch an *offline attack*. In this case they will have the chance to make many more attempts, so they will probably try using dictionaries (perhaps in several languages), name lists, character substitution algorithms on dictionary words – such as replacing the letter s with the digit 5 – and possibly pure brute-force attempts. It is the possibility of such offline attacks that motivates the recommendation to use a long password that includes a mixture of upper-case and lower-case letters and at least one digit, since this guarantees that the password will not appear in a dictionary or name list. It is worth noting that attackers know about character substitutions and the habit of adding a single digit to the end of a word, so any digits should be placed in random positions. The use of upper case should also be randomized and not restricted to initial letters.

Sometimes, Web applications will force users creating accounts to choose passwords which are subject to some constraints intended to make them more secure against offline attacks. The trouble is, as you probably know from experience, that this forces people to use passwords which are hard to remember, with the result that they may write them down, possibly on a sticky note attached to their computer screen, where they might easily be seen by other people. Another consideration which may influence you when deciding whether to enforce strong passwords for users signing up to your application is the users' convenience and patience. If you are running a Web-based service which requires customers to sign up and create an account before they can do anything or pay for it, you will want to make the process of account creation as quick and easy as possible, otherwise you may drive away business. If somebody's first choice of password is rejected, there is a high probability that they will just give up, unless your service is compelling and has no rivals. If more than one attempt to create a password is rejected, they will almost certainly leave and never return. So although requiring strong passwords may be good security, it isn't always good for business. As we shall see, security must often be a matter for compromise or trade-off in practice.

It is worth imposing a minimum length on users' passwords, as very short passwords are inevitably insecure and will put the users' data at risk. Users should be encouraged implicitly to use long passwords – for example, by providing a wide text field to enter them in. Do not impose a maximum length, unless there is a limit on the size of request data your application and Web server can handle. If passwords are stored securely using a cryptographic hash, as we will describe in the next section, the amount of storage required for the password is independent of its length, so no space in the database is saved by insisting on short passwords.

Storing Passwords

Keeping passwords safe is a high priority, as they are the primary defence against unauthorized access to most systems. A password is a persistent piece of information, which must be kept somewhere so that it can be checked every time a user tries to log in. The passwords needed for logging in to the server host itself are most often stored in a designated file, whose location is dependent on the type of operating system. (Password storage on the server host is described in more detail in another book in this series, *A Web Developer's Guide to Securing a Server.*) Most Web applications will store their passwords in a database. Typically, in a relational database a table called users or customers will have a field for the password. A corresponding collection of documents would be used in a "NoSQL" database. In every case, the data should be protected as far as possible, but it is foolish to assume that an attacker will never be able to gain access to the password file or users data.

To minimize the consequences of unauthorized access to passwords, you should never store users' passwords in unencrypted form or use a reversible algorithm to encrypt them.

This rule is so important that we are going to repeat it. Never store users' passwords in unencrypted form or use a reversible algorithm to encrypt them. Instead, always compute a ***cryptographic hash*** of the password and store that. That is, a strong encryption algorithm should be used to encrypt the password in such a way that decrypting it is not feasible. (For more details, consult the *Notes on Cryptography* at the end of this book.) Then, when a user attempts to log in, compute a hash from the credentials they submit and compare that with the stored value, as illustrated in Figure 1. It is true that there is a non-zero probability of two different passwords yielding the same hash value, but the possibility is so slight that for practical purposes it is safe to assume that if the hashed values match, the user has provided the correct password. By definition, a cryptographic hash function makes finding a string that is hashed to the same value as some other string computationally infeasible, so a collision between hash values would only occur as the result of a remotely improbable coincidence.

The effectiveness of online attacks can be reduced by using a cryptographic hash function that is slow to execute. Of course, it should not be so slow that legitimate logins take an excessive amount of time, but people are prepared to wait a couple of seconds, which would be sufficient time for thousands of automatic login attempts if the delay were not imposed. A hashing algorithm that was deliberately designed to slow down online

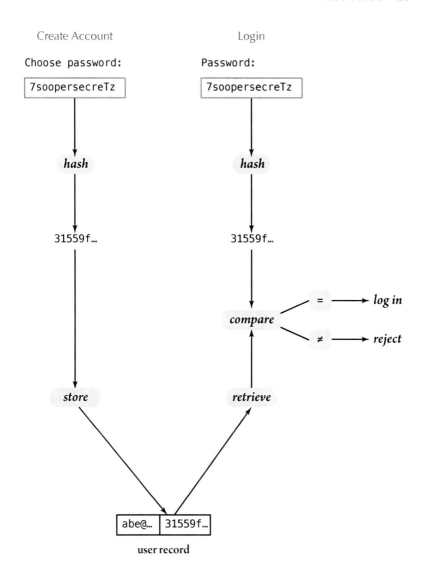

Figure 1. *Storing and checking hashed passwords*

password-cracking attempts is **bcrypt**. The hashing algorithm in bcrypt is deliberately made slow. The extent of this slowing down can be controlled by a "cost factor", which is provided as a parameter to the algorithm. As computer hardware gets faster, the cost factor can be increased to compensate.

An important (and desirable) consequence of applying a cryptographic hash function to passwords before storing them is that it is impossible to retrieve the original plaintext password to send to any user who claims to have forgotten their password. This provides extra security, as it prevents plaintext passwords from being sent by email, or to users who may be imposters, but it means that more imaginative procedures have to be used to deal with genuine cases of forgotten passwords, as we will describe in a later section. It follows that if a Web site does provide a facility for sending passwords to users who claim to have forgotten them, that site must be storing passwords in a retrievable and therefore insecure fashion. If you need to create an account on such a site as a user, make sure that you do not use the same password anywhere else.

Hashing the password ensures that if an attacker gains access to the file or database they cannot just read the plaintext password, but this still leaves the possibility of offline attacks against the encrypted data.

Suppose you had got hold of the database for a Web application, including the users' data, and that you had a good idea of which hashing algorithm had been used on the passwords. (This can often be guessed by looking at the length of the stored hash value.) If you wanted to discover users' passwords, the obvious thing to do would be to take your dictionary, list of common passwords, list of names and any other words you thought might be passwords, and work through them, computing the hash for each one and comparing it with the values stored in the table. If you had a network of fast computers (or special-purpose hardware, if you were serious), you might be able to work through them in a feasible time. However, there is a much more efficient way to proceed. You could run through your dictionary and other word lists once, computing the hash of each potential password, and store the results in a table together with the corresponding plaintext. (You could usefully do this for each of the commonly used hashing algorithms.) Then, when you obtained a database containing passwords, you would simply compare the stored password hashes with the entries in your table. If you sort the table by hash value, the look-up can be done very quickly. However, the tables for any substantial list of potential passwords are huge.

This approach to password cracking has been made more effective by a method of ordering passwords and their hashes that allows hashes to be organized as chains, such that all the values in each chain can be inferred from the first and last entries alone. The resulting table, called a *rainbow table*, can be much smaller than a full table of strings and their hashes, which means that many more precomputed values can be stored, and the attack need not be limited to a relatively small dictionary or word list. An attempt to discover passwords using a rainbow table is known as a *rainbow attack*. Rainbow tables and programs to generate them are readily available.

Fortunately, rainbow attacks can be quite easily foiled. Before computing the hash of a password, a random string called a *salt* is added to the end of it. The salt for each password should be unique. It is generated the first time the password is stored, and is kept with the hashed password, so that it can be appended to any string presented as a password during login. (See Figure 2.) There is no need to hash the salt or do anything to conceal it. Its only purpose is to ensure that the hash stored for a particular password will not always be the same. In other words, the value stored for a password such as 7soopersecreTz in the users table of an application that uses password salting will not be the same as the value stored for the string 7soopersecreTz in a rainbow table, because the value stored in the users table is actually the hash of something like 7soopersecreTzqs5RJFc82iNF, where the suffix qs5RJFc82iNF is the salt.

Salting passwords has additional benefits. In the absence of salt, it would always be possible to determine whether two users had the same password, or whether the same person was using the same password on multiple Web sites or services. This would mean that having obtained someone's password once, perhaps by phishing for it, and having identified its hashed value, it would be possible to determine when that same password was being used by other users, or by the same user on other sites, just by looking at their passwords' hash values. It would then be simple to obtain access to the associated accounts. Salting the password prevents this, because in effect it generates new passwords every time, even if the passwords actually entered by users are identical.

To demonstrate the ideas we have discussed so far, we will develop an implementation of a data model suitable for storing and subsequently checking users' credentials using a scheme such as the one shown in Figure 2, which uses salted passwords. The code illustrates some extra points that must be considered when creating users' accounts.

An email address will be used to identify each user. This avoids their having to think up and remember a user name as well as a password. As email addresses are unique, using them to identify users should also avoid the problem of two people choosing the same user name. In most cases, a Web application will need to record every user's email address anyway, as a means of getting in touch with them, so email addresses provide a neat way of identifying users without burdening them with unnecessary red tape.

We will store the data in a conventional relational database. To start with, the users table must be created. It simply records each user's email address and the password hash. The bcrypt module combines the salt and hash into a single value, so there is no need to store the salt explicitly.

Our users table will be mapped to objects in our program, using the persistent_objects module described in the *Introduction*. Like any other table used in this way, the records in the users table include time stamps and an integer field to hold a unique identifier for each record. This field makes certain operations on the data more convenient. In particular, it allows a user's email address to be changed without deleting the record and creating a new one. In a real application it might be necessary or desirable to store some extra data about each user, but for now we will only consider the values needed for authentication.

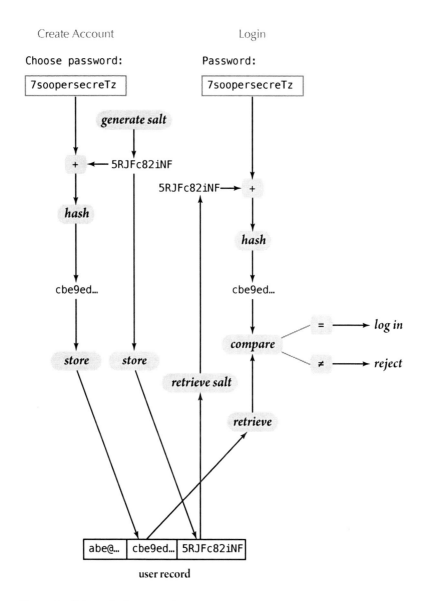

Figure 2. *Using salted passwords*

bcrypt Hash Values

The bcrypt module produces values that are 60 bytes long. The hash value itself occupies 184 bits and the salt occupies 128 bits. Both of these values are *base 64* encoded, which leads to a string of 53 ASCII characters, with the salt appearing first. This string is preceded by the characters $2a$ which serve to identify the hashing algorithm and format, then two digits giving the cost factor, and another $ sign. Here is a typical value produced by the bcrypt module:

```
$2a$10$mxyTzgdoBszdOTAtsYmkmONJ8lXKeE5t2sljG5o/
ermTvrfrg0B1O
```

(We have been obliged to split the value across two lines here, but it is really a single string with no embedded return character.) As you should be able to appreciate, it is simple to extract the salt from this combined value when it is needed, even though it is not stored explicitly in a separate field in the users table.

It would be confusing to have more than one account for the same email address. Allowing duplicate accounts would also make it impossible to impose limitations on the resources that an individual could use. Therefore, the values stored in the field for email addresses should be unique – that is, each value may only occur once in the table. A check can be performed whenever an account is created to ensure that no account for the given email address already exists, but as an added precaution the database itself can check the constraint. This is done by creating an index on the field with the keyword UNIQUE. An exception will be raised if any attempt is made to insert duplicate email addresses into the database by any means.

Listing 2 shows the schema of the users table. The table must be created using a database client before any account data can be stored.

Listing 3, displayed on the following few pages, shows a model for working with user account data stored in a relational database. The complete model

Listing 2
```
1  CREATE TABLE "users" (
2    "id" INTEGER PRIMARY KEY AUTOINCREMENT NOT NULL,
3    "email_address" VARCHAR(255) NOT NULL,
4    "password_hash" VARCHAR(60) NOT NULL,
5    "created_at" datetime,
6    "updated_at" datetime
7  );
8  CREATE UNIQUE INDEX "index_users_on_email_address"
9    ON "users" ("email_address");
```

includes the standard methods and properties for mapping between objects and database entities, as described in the *Introduction*. This code is not concerned with security, so we have just indicated its presence by comments.

Our module for user accounts exports a single function (on line 1) that takes a DBWrapper object as its argument. This function returns a constructor for User objects on line 91 of this listing. (If you download the complete source, you will find that the line numbers do not match the listings in this chapter, because we have elided extraneous details here in the interests of readability.)

If db is a DBWrapper object, it can be passed as an argument when the User module is required:

```
var User = require('./models/users.js')(db);
```

Since the value returned by the module is a closure, the DBWrapper object passed as an argument is available to all the methods attached to the User prototype within it, allowing them to perform database operations.

The constructor that the module exports is defined on lines 16–22. It may take an argument consisting of a hash of options. This hash is intended to consist of the values for the email address and password of a new user. If the options are provided, these values are assigned to suitably named

Listing 3

```
1  module.exports = function(db) {
2
3    var bcrypt = require('bcrypt');
4
5    var weakPassword = function(pw) {
6     return !pw || pw.length < 8 ||
7     !(/\d/).test(pw) || !(/[a-z]/).test(pw) ||
8     !(/[A-Z]/).test(pw);
9    };
10
11   var validEmail = function(e) {
12      return e && e.length < 255 && e.length >= 6 &&
13      (/^[^@\s]+@([-a-z0-9]+\.)+([a-z]{2,4}|museum)$/i).test(e);
14   };
15
16   var User = function(options) {
17    if (options) {
18      this.email = options.email;
19      this.password = options.password;
20      this._isNew = true;
21    }
22   };
23
24   // Persistence rubric, table and db properties
25
26   var persistentUser =
27            require('../lib/persistent_objects')(User);
28
29   User.prototype.save = persistentUser.save(
30    function(u) { return u._passwordOK && u._emailOK; },
31     'You must provide a valid email address and password');
32
33   // Other persistence methods: destroy and count
34
35   // Standard properties: id, updatedAt, createdAt and iNew
36
```

```
37   // Accessor properties
38
39   Object.defineProperty(User.prototype, 'email', {
40     get: function(){
41       return this._emailAddress;
42     },
43     set: function(e) {
44       this._emailOK = validEmail(e);
45       this._emailAddress = e.toLowerCase();
46     }
47   });
48
49   Object.defineProperty(User.prototype, 'password', {
50     set: function(pw) {
51       this._passwordOK = !weakPassword(pw);
52       this._passwordHash = bcrypt.hashSync(pw,
53                           bcrypt.genSaltSync(10));
54     }
55   });
56
57   User.prototype.checkPassword = function(pw) {
58     return bcrypt.compareSync(pw, this._passwordHash);
59   };
60
61   // Static methods
62
63   User.find = function(field, value, callback) {
64     persistentUser.findOneObject(field + ' = ?', [value],
65             function(err, theUser) {
66               if (!err && theUser)
67                 theUser._emailOK = theUser._passwordOK = true;
68               callback(err, theUser);
69             });
70   };
71
72   User.findByEmail = function(e, callback) {
73     User.find('email_address', e, callback);
74   };
75
```

```
76   User.findById = function(i, callback) {
77     User.find('id', i, callback);
78   };
79
80   User.checkCredentials = function(e, pw, callback) {
81     this.findByEmail(e, function(err, u){
82       if (u == null)
83         err = new Error('unknown user');
84       else
85         if (!u.checkPassword(pw))
86           err = new Error('incorrect password');
87       callback(err, u);
88     });
89   };
90
91   return User;
92 }
```

properties of the object being constructed (lines 18 and 19). In accordance with the convention we are using for persistent objects, these are "private" properties, which are included in the persistentProperties array. Also following our conventions, a flag is set to indicate that the object has not been saved to the database yet (line 20). New User objects can therefore be created by passing a suitable hash to the constructor returned from our module. For instance,

```
var gwendolen = new User({email:'gwendolen@abelardos.com.fd',
             password: 'iam2Secret'});
```

Normally, the values passed to the constructor would be obtained from an HTTP request, which would probably have been sent by submitting a sign-up form, as we will demonstrate later.

The email and password properties are the most important parts of a User object. Both of them are *accessor properties*, not simple data properties. Accessor properties, introduced in ECMAScript 5, allow the programmer to define get and set functions (also known as getters and setters) that may perform some computation as well as retrieving or storing a value when the property is used or assigned to, respectively. Accessor properties may be defined by calling the Object.defineProperty method.

The email property is defined on lines 39–47. The actual value of the email address is stored in a private data property called _emailAddress. Hence, the get function returns the value of this property.

The set function first ensures that the value being assigned could be a valid email address, by calling the validEmail function, which we will discuss shortly. Then it converts the value to lower case. Strictly speaking, the local part of an email address (the part before the @ character) is case sensitive, although the domain name is not, so Abe@abelardos.com.fd could be a different address from abe@abelardos.com.fd, for example. This rarely happens in practice, and having two users with email addresses that are identical except for case is likely to cause confusion, so we normalize the entire email address to lower case before storing it. Calling the String.toLowerCase method in the setter ensures that the normalization is always done.

The password property on lines 49–55 is critical. It ensures that passwords are always salted and encrypted before being stored. The setter includes a rudimentary check that the password is strong enough. It then performs the essential salting and encryption. The bcrypt module, required on line 3, makes this easy. It exports methods for generating a salt, for encrypting a password, and for comparing a password with a stored hash. Recent versions of the bcrypt module export two sets of methods – one set that performs the operations asynchronously, and another that is synchronous. Since we are using bcrypt specifically to slow down the checking of passwords, it would be silly to perform the operations asynchronously – we positively want the operations to block. The synchronous methods are identified by being suffixed with Sync. As we remarked earlier, the salt and hash are combined into a single value, which also incorporates the number of rounds used for the encryption. The bcrypt.genSaltSync method takes the number of rounds as an argument; it incorporates the value in its result as a way of passing it on to `bcrypt.hashSync`. The nested calls on lines 52 and 53 generate the salt, hash it and the password, and return the combined value to be stored. We will demonstrate shortly how this stored value can be used to check passwords entered during login attempts. There is no get function for this property because it is only necessary to compare the password's hashed value with another hash. It should never be necessary – and is anyway impossible – to retrieve the stored password.

In the `User` constructor, the values provided for the email address and password are assigned to the `email` and `password` accessor properties, respectively, not to the private properties that store the data. This ensures that the assignments invoke the setters, so the values are checked for validity, the email address is lower-cased, and the password is salted and hashed when the object is constructed, all as required.

The function for validating email addresses is defined on lines 11–14. It ensures that the address's length is within reasonable bounds, and matches it against a regular expression that performs a simple check for the essential elements of a valid email address. This check should be sufficient for applications whose security is not critical, but you should realize that the only way to determine whether an email address is a real one is by sending a message to it and getting a reply. Even then, you cannot be sure that you are not dealing with one of the many disposable email address services that exist (ostensibly to combat spam). You can try rejecting addresses whose second part matches one of a list of known disposable domains, but such a list will almost certainly be incomplete and rapidly out of date.

For applications whose security is essential, it is wise to modify the account creation process so that instead of creating an account immediately, an email message containing a URL is sent to the address provided. This URL should incorporate a unique validation token and point to a page with a second simple HTML form that must be filled in to activate the account. We will not show the implementation of this check here, as a similar scheme is described later in this chapter, in the section on resetting passwords.

Validating Email Addresses

This isn't as easy as it sounds. There is an official IETF standard defining the allowable syntax for email addresses, but it is very complicated. It allows many addresses that would not be accepted by some email clients, and others that, while syntactically well-formed, could not be real email addresses because they belong to nonexistent domains or do not correspond to any actual mailbox. Although you can find regular expressions which parse all and only the strings defined by the relevant standard, it is more common and practical to use a simpler expression, similar to the one in our User model, which just makes sure that the address looks as if it consists of two parts separated by an @ sign. If it is important that the email address be truly valid, a supplementary check that includes sending a message to it and receiving a reply must be performed.

The first part of an address is the individual's name (officially known as the "local part"). The format of this part is determined in practice by the system hosting the corresponding mailbox, so the standard is extremely liberal in what is permitted here. The sub-expression [^@\s]+ matches any non-empty string containing any characters except @ and white space, which is not what the standard stipulates, but does allow most email addresses found in practice and rejects the worst malformed ones. After the @ character, the second part of the address comprises several names, made up of letters, hyphens and digits, separated by dots. This part is matched by the sub-expression ([-a-z0-9]+\.)+. After this, the ending of the address must match ([a-z]{2,4}|museum), because the last part of the host name will be a TLD (top-level domain). A careful check would enumerate all the existing TLD abbreviations here. However, that list is extensive and liable to change, so, apart from the single current TLD that is longer than four characters (.museum), we just allow any string of between 2 and 4 letters. This allows all country TLDs and the established global TLDs like .com and .info.

In JavaScript regexps, ^ matches the beginning of the string and $ the end, so wrapping the regexp in these ensures that the entire string matches the pattern for an email address and that there are no extra bits at the beginning or end. Adding the qualifier /i after the expression makes the comparison case-independent, so any mixture of upper- and lower-case letters is accepted, as it should be.

ICANN's new procedures for approving gTLDs, announced in 2011, mean that in future there will probably be many more valid domain names, and many TLDs beside .museum will be longer than four characters. New domain names may also use the full range of Unicode characters. Coupled with the use of non-ASCII characters in the local part, this will make checking the syntactical validity of email addresses even more difficult.

Earlier, we emphasized that security depends on users choosing passwords that are hard to guess. If a user's password is compromised, not only their security, but that of other users of the site may be jeopardized, so there is a case for trying to enforce strong passwords. The most convenient place to do this is in the browser, when the user is choosing their password during the sign-up process. Some users still disable JavaScript, though, and it is possible that, for good or bad reasons, someone may try to create an account using a program other than a browser. As with all other validations, if it is considered that passwords should be checked for strength, any validation performed in the browser must be augmented with a further check at the server end. The function defined on lines 5–9 checks for some rudimentary properties of a weak password that should be rejected – if it's empty or fewer than 8 characters long, does not include at least one digit, or at least one upper-case letter and one lower-case letter. Writing a single regular expression that checks all these conditions is possible, but requires ingenuity and the use of the ugly lookahead operators. Checking each condition individually with separate expressions is trivial, so we do that. The amount of checking that it is reasonable to impose on users is a matter for debate.

In both the email and password properties there is no easy way of dealing with invalid data inside the setter, except perhaps by raising an exception. We prefer to assign the result of the validation to private properties, _emailOK and _passwordOK, and check their values when an attempt is made to insert the object into the database. That is, we allow objects to be constructed with invalid email addresses and weak passwords, but never let such data be stored permanently.

User objects must be saved to the database explicitly by calling the save method defined on lines 29–31. The value assigned to User.save is the function returned from the save method of our persistent_objects module, with a callback that examines the values of _passwordOK and _emailOK to see whether the values in the object are valid, and a suitable message to be used if one or both of them is invalid.

It has to be possible to retrieve data after it has been stored. We define findByEmail and findById methods to retrieve a record with a given email address or id value, respectively, in terms of a general find method, shown on lines 63–70, which takes the name of a field and a value and constructs the where part of a prepared SQL select query to persistentUser.findOneObject, in the manner described in the *Introduction*. We also pass a callback, defined on lines 65–69, that sets the internal flags to record that the email address and password in the object constructed from the retrieved data are valid, and then pass that object to whatever callback was supplied to the find method.

The main purpose of User objects is to provide a means of checking a set of credentials and discovering whether or not they identify a registered user. This check is needed whenever somebody attempts to log in to a user account. The email address and password stored in the database provide enough information for the checking to be performed. In the next chapter we will describe how the appropriate interface for users to log in can be provided. Here we will assume that two strings have been obtained, one claiming to be the email address of a registered user, and the other claiming to be that user's password. We need to determine whether these strings are legitimate, using the values stored in the database.

The checking process involves determining whether the email address provided during the login attempt identifies an existing user account and, if it does, checking whether the password that is being supplied for login matches the password record for that account. The static method checkCredentials defined on lines 80–89 does this. This method has to be static (that is, a property of the constructor, not of its prototype), because when it is called, no User object has been retrieved from the database. Retrieving the object is done by the findByEmail method described earlier, with the anonymous function defined on lines 81–88 being passed to it as the callback argument. If there is no database error during the retrieval, and the email address does identify a stored account, the callback's second argument will be a User object. (In the conventional way, the first argument is used for an Error object if a database error occurs.)

If the second argument is null, the email address did not identify a user with an account, so an Error object is created and assigned to err, to record this fact. If the second argument is not null, the password can be checked. This is done by calling the User object's method checkPassword, which is defined on lines 57–59. The method body is trivial, because the compareSync method of bcrypt extracts the salt from its second argument and uses it to generate a hash from its first argument. The two hashes are then compared. These operations are all synchronous. Hence, simply calling this method, as we do on line 58, is sufficient to discover whether the argument pw matches the password whose hash is stored in the User object, and the result can be returned immediately.

If the password check fails, an Error object is created and assigned to err. Hence, on line 87, the value of err will only be null if a User object was retrieved using the email address supplied and its password matched that which was given. The retrieved value (which may be null if the lookup failed) is passed to the callback, together with any Error object resulting from the database lookup or a failure of the email or password checks.

The callback can then examine its first argument to determine whether to allow the user access to the account, or whether to deal with the failed login attempt in a suitable way. We will describe what needs to be done in each case in the next chapter.

Key Points

- Most applications need to restrict certain operations to authorized users only.

- Accounts allow data to be associated with individual users. Passwords are used to restrict access to accounts.

- Always set your own password when you install any system that sets a default. Make sure any package you create for others to install will not work until a password has been set explicitly.

- The hardness of a password is not an absolute property, but depends on the methods attackers use in attempts to crack it.

- Long passwords consisting of a mixture of upper and lower case letters and digits can withstand most casual attacks.

- If attackers obtain the file or database in which encrypted passwords are stored, they can launch an offline attack using dictionaries, name lists, character substitution algorithms on dictionary words, and pure brute-force attempts.

- Never store users' passwords in unencrypted form or use a reversible algorithm to encrypt them. Always compute a cryptographic hash of the password and store that instead.

- The effectiveness of online attacks can be reduced by using a cryptographic hash function that is slow to execute.

- Rainbow attacks make use of pre-computed tables of hashed passwords to speed up the process of trying passwords.

- Adding a random salt to a password before hashing it will foil rainbow attacks.

- Perform rudimentary validation on the user's email address and ensure the password is reasonably hard before storing the record for a new account.

Managing Accounts

The User model provides a safe way of storing users' email addresses and passwords, but a model isn't much use on its own. Accounts must actually be created, email addresses and passwords may need changing from time to time, and sometimes accounts will have to be deleted. In general, two different cases must be considered. On most sites that provide accounts, users must be able to create accounts, edit their details, and delete their own accounts. At the same time, the site's administrators must be able to perform certain privileged operations, such as suspending or deleting the accounts of users who have broken the terms and conditions of use. In this chapter we will only consider the case of users creating and managing their own accounts.

Creating and Updating Accounts

Most Web applications that let users create accounts provide a sign-up page for the purpose. Figure 3 is a simplified example with the minimum of features. This model only stores email and password values.

New Account

Please fill in all the fields below.

Your email address

Choose a password

Confirm the password

Passwords must be at least 8 characters long, containing at least one upper-case letter, lower-case letter and a digit that isn't on the end.

Create the account

Figure 3. *A form for creating a simple user account*

Providing the values that are entered pass the validations, a new User object should be created when this form is submitted. It is common to require the user to type the password a second time to confirm it, as this helps prevent the situation that may arise if a user mistypes their intended password when creating an account. If the User object is created with the wrong password, the user will be unable to log in when they try to use the password they believe they had originally entered.

The value typed in an HTML input element whose type attribute is set to password is *masked* – that is, the characters entered by the user are displayed as a row of bullets or asterisks, to prevent the password being read by passers-by. However, the masking of passwords also prevents their being read by the user, so that mistyped passwords go unnoticed. The use of a password confirmation field is not an infallible safeguard against mistyping, but it may help. Recently, some influential user interface experts have questioned the use of masked password fields, on the grounds that they offer little security but prevent valuable interface feedback. We will return to this issue in the next chapter when we consider signing in, but note meanwhile that one advantage of not masking the password field during account creation is that the confirmation becomes redundant.

There are some special precautions which should be taken in connection with the operations that change or delete an existing account. To begin with, it should only be possible for a user to edit the details of their own account. This is an instance of a general requirement that certain operations should only be permitted to a user who has identified themselves to the system – that is, who has logged in. We will devote the next two chapters to describing mechanisms for logging in and determining which user sent a particular request. For now, we assume that we have some way of doing so.

It is particularly important to ensure, so far as you can, that nobody is able to change a user's password except the user whose password it is. Suppose a user logs in to the application using a shared computer then, for some reason, leaves the computer without logging out. Somebody else can then come along and use their account. You can certainly argue that it is the user's responsibility to make sure that this doesn't happen, but it is prudent to try to minimize the damage that might result if it does. For this reason, a user should be required to enter their password again when they attempt to change the email address or password for an account, as illustrated in Figure 4, even though they must already be logged in to have reached this form. This prevents anyone who does not know the current password from performing these operations. (At this point we are not considering the case of a user who needs to set a new password because they have forgotten the old one. That is a problematic situation which requires special treatment, as we will describe later.) When a password is being changed, it is usual to require confirmation of the new one, for the same reason that confirmation of the password is required when an account is first created.

Change Your Email Address or Password

Leave this field alone if you only want to change your password.

New email address   abe@abelardos.com.fd

You must enter your password to make any changes.

Your current password

Leave these next two fields blank if you only want to change your email address.

Choose a new password

Confirm the new password

Passwords must be at least 8 characters long, containing at least one upper-case letter, lower-case letter and a digit that isn't on the end.

Update

Figure 4. *A form for updating a user account*

Deletion of an account should also require the user's password, as a minimum precaution. In many cases it may be considered necessary to require explicit confirmation from the user before deleting the account. If deleting an account means losing access to remotely stored data or to entitlements to downloads or services, for example, you should make sure that the user appreciates the consequences, and take every possible step to ensure that the person deleting the account has the authority to do so. Confirmation can usually be obtained in a similar way to that in which the creation of an important account may be confirmed – that is, by sending an email to the recorded address. This email should contain a unique URL incorporating a special token. The account can only be deleted by sending a request to that precise URL. For accounts whose deletion has few consequences, it may be adequate to use JavaScript to pop up a dialogue asking the user to confirm that they really want to delete the account.

Modern Web applications are usually constructed following the Model-View-Controller (MVC) pattern. We have already constructed a model, which deals with data manipulation. In Web applications, views are HTML pages and forms for displaying data and interacting with users. Controllers receive and interpret HTTP requests, invoke model operations to manipulate the data, and send HTTP responses to display views.

We will demonstrate the controller for a basic application that enables users to create and manage accounts. The controller, shown in Listing 4, uses the Express framework. (Further information about Express can be found at expressjs.com and on this series' companion Web site at www.websecuritytopics.info.)

The controller module is a function that takes the User constructor as an argument so that the methods defined in it can refer to User objects. It exports an object consisting of six methods, which between them carry out the operations necessary for creating, updating and deleting user accounts. We have included a show method which displays the current user's account details. In our example, the only data displayed is the email address, but any additional user profile data could be displayed here as well.

Each method in an Express controller takes two arguments, conventionally called req and res, which are objects representing the incoming HTTP request and the response to be sent back. The framework defines methods and properties on these objects, which allow the controller methods to examine the request and create the response. It also arranges for the request headers to appear as properties of req and places any request data in req.body. Following convention, we name the form fields for the user's email address and password user[email] and user[password] and Express obligingly provides an object req.body.user, with properties email and password. This method of making data from the request body available to controller methods in arrays is used throughout all Express applications.

Commonly, middleware adds extra properties to the request. In our application, we use middleware to retrieve various resources required by a request and attach the retrieved data to the req object. In particular, we will show in the next chapter how we can retrieve a User object for the user associated with the current request. This is assigned to req.currentUser, and you will see that this value is used in several places in this controller.

Express's routing system invokes the controller's methods in response to HTTP requests. The comment line above each method's definition indicates the form of request it responds to. Experienced Web application developers will recognize that the combination of paths and HTTP verbs we have used to select methods to execute follows the RESTful pattern of routing, with a user being considered a singular resource. That is, URLs do not include an id value to select a user. This is to ensure that each user can only edit or delete their own account. We will return to this way of organizing URLs in the chapter on *Authorization*.

If you are not yet used to this style of programming, the extensive use of anonymous functions as callbacks may make the code hard to follow at first, but the methods exported by the controller are actually very simple. Those which are invoked by GET requests just display a view, by calling the render method provided by Express. Data for the current user is passed to

Listing 4

```
1   module.exports = function(User) {
2
3    return {
4     // GET /user/new
5     new: function(req, res){
6      res.render('users/new',
7       {title: 'Sign up',
8        u: null,
9        layout: 'blank-layout'
10      });
11     },
12
13     // POST /user
14     create: function(req, res){
15      var userData = req.body.user;
16      var theUser = new User(userData);
17      var badSignUpForm = function(e) {
18       req.flash('error', e);
19       res.render('users/new',
20        {title: 'Error in sign-up form',
21         u: theUser,
22         layout: 'blank-layout'
23       });
24      };
25      if (userData.password == userData.confirm) {
26       theUser.save(function(err) {
27        if (err)
28         badSignUpForm(err.message);
29        else {
30         req.flash('info', 'Your account has been created');
31         req.userId = req.session.userId = theUser.id;
32         res.redirect('/user', { title: 'Your account',
33                                 user: theUser});
34        }
35       });
36      }
```

```
37     else
38       badSignUpForm('Your password and its confirmation must
match');
39     },
40
41     // GET /user
42     show: function(req, res){
43       res.render('users/show', {
44         title: 'Your account',
45         user: req.currentUser
46       });
47     },
48
49     // GET /user/edit
50     edit: function(req, res){
51       res.render('users/edit', {
52         title: 'Edit your account',
53         user: req.currentUser
54       });
55     },
56
57     // PUT /user
58     update: function(req, res){
59       var theUser = req.currentUser;
60       var badEditForm = function(e) {
61         req.flash('error', e);
62         res.render('users/edit',
63           {title: 'Error making changes',
64            u: theUser,
65            layout: 'blank-layout'
66         });
67       };
68       var changes = false;
69       var newUserData = req.body.user;
70       if (theUser.checkPassword(newUserData.old_password)) {
71         if (newUserData.email &&
72             newUserData.email != theUser.email) {
73           theUser.email = newUserData.email;
74           changes = true;
75         }
```

```
76      if (newUserData.password)
77        if (newUserData.password == newUserData.confirm) {
78          theUser.password = newUserData.password;
79          changes = true;
80        }
81        else
82          badEditForm('Your new password and its confirmation
must match');
83      }
84      else
85        badEditForm('Incorrect password – you must enter your old
password to make these changes.')
86      if (changes) {
87        theUser.save(function(err) {
88          if (err)
89            badEditForm(err.message);
90          else {
91            req.flash('info', 'Your account details have been
changed');
92            res.render('users/show',
93                        { title: 'Your account', user: theUser});
94          }
95        });
96      }
97    },
98
99    // DELETE /user
100   destroy: function(req, res){
101     var e = req.currentUser.email;
102     User.destroy(e);
103     req.session.destroy();
104     res.render('users/delete', {
105       title: 'Your account has been deleted',
106       email: e,
107       layout: 'blank-layout'
108     })
109   }
110 }
111 }
```

render to be incorporated in the view. The create and update methods are slightly more complex, but only because they have to carry out checks on the data received in the request.

One check that is not included in Listing 4 is a check for duplicated email addresses. As we explained when describing the User model, the unique index on the email_address column in the users table ensures that there can only ever be one record with a particular email address. Attempting to insert or update a record with an email address that is already present in the table will cause an error, which will be passed to the callback which was the argument to the save method, and ultimately displayed to the user. The message incorporated in this Error object is succinct and expressed in terms of the database error that provoked it (for example, in the case of an SQLite database, SQLITE_CONSTRAINT: constraint failed), so it would be quite bewildering to most users. As a friendlier means of dealing with this eventuality, we make an explicit check beforehand and generate our own message, as shown in Listing 5. The method reject_duplicate_email exported by the module defined in this listing is applied as middleware to the routes for the create and update controller methods. You can see the details of how this is done by downloading the example code. If you object to the additional database access required by this method, you could perhaps catch the database error and replace it with a friendlier message, providing you were certain which constraint had been violated.

The views we have used to display and collect data are trivial, so we won't show the code for them here. They can be organized and formatted in any appropriate way.

Suitable links are needed to provide a means of accessing these controller methods. It is common to include at least one link labelled "Sign Up" or "Create An Account", often on the site's home page, with its href attribute pointing to the URL /user/new, so that clicking on it will display the form shown earlier. On many sites, particularly those whose purpose is to provide a service that is paid for, such links are displayed prominently on many pages. It is also common to add a "My Account" link, which is shown

Listing 5

```
1 module.exports = function(User) {
2   return {
3     reject_duplicate_email: function(req, res, next) {
4       var userData = req.body.user;
5       User.findByEmail(userData.email, function(err, u) {
6         if (u) {
7           req.flash('error', 'An account already exists with
email address ' + u.email);
8           res.redirect('back');
9         }
10        else
11          next();
12      });
13    }
14  };
15 }
```

on every page when a user is logged in. This link can point to the URL /user so that it invokes the show action to give access to a page displaying the account details (which normally include more information than we have provided for in our example). This page is a possible place to include the links to the update and delete operations. However, this is just one way of organizing things, and other arrangements are possible.

Submitting the forms to create or update an account means sending the user's email address and password over the network. Both the form and the submitted data should ideally be sent over **HTTPS**, to eliminate the possibility of *man-in-the-middle* attacks. (We explain this in more detail in *A Web Developer's Guide to Secure Communication*, another short book in this series.) If you want to embed a small login form on every page, perhaps revealed in situ by clicking the "Sign Up" link, you should consider serving the entire site over HTTPS. You should always remember that even if you believe a user whose password is stolen will not suffer from any damage done on your Web site, they may be using the same password on other sites where an attacker who obtains their password could do much more harm.

There is one more very important precaution that must be taken in connection with these operations on user accounts (and with logging in). Web servers and Web applications maintain extensive logs recording request data. These log files are often less securely protected than other data held on the server host, so that it is easier for an attacker to gain access to them than to the password database. The standard logs created by the server itself are unlikely to include any sensitive information, but some Web application frameworks maintain their own log files. (Ruby on Rails does this, for instance, and the data written to the log by default includes the values of all parameters sent in a request, including passwords.) This is highly undesirable, as it means that unencrypted passwords can be read by the site administrator, or by anyone else who obtains access to the logs. Passwords and their confirmations should therefore be excluded from logging. Node.js and Express do not log requests by default, but if you decide to implement your own logger, remember to make it possible to exclude not just the password, but any password confirmation too. Be particularly careful if you decide to record all attempts to log in.

Preventing the Creation of Bad Accounts

Web sites that rely on content contributed by their users – forums, blogs, social networking sites, and so on – usually require anyone who wishes to post content on the site to create an account first. One reason for doing this is to prevent anonymous users from abusing the service by posting spam or planting "drive-by downloads", or doing other undesirable things without being identified. In response, spammers and their more sinister colleagues have developed programs that can traverse the Web automatically, creating accounts wherever they find the opportunity. Such a program is trivial to write. All it has to do is recognize a form that looks as if it is intended for creating accounts, then fill in an email address, perhaps a user name, a password, and its confirmation. Subsequently, another program can return to the site, log in using those credentials, and post undesirable or dangerous content. The creation of accounts by malicious programs is only likely to be a problem when accounts can be created for free, but this is the case in most forums and blogs, where it can lead to serious problems and allow spam to swamp legitimate content if contributions are not moderated.

Various tools and strategies have been proposed for preventing programs from creating accounts in this way. The most widely deployed has been the **CAPTCHA**. The term is said to stand for "Completely Automated Public Turing test to tell Computers and Humans Apart", though this is obviously contrived to fit the play on the word "capture". Like the classic Turing Test, the purpose of a CAPTCHA is to distinguish between real people and machines that are behaving like people. The reason for trying to do so is quite different in this case, though.

You have probably encountered CAPTCHAs yourself. They generally consist of an image of a few letters and digits that have been distorted in some way or placed on a confusing background. This is supposed to make it hard – ideally impossible – for an optical character recognition (OCR) algorithm to identify the characters. A person with good sight should be able to read the characters without too much difficulty, so the form displaying the CAPTCHA has a box into which the characters must be copied. Figure 5 shows a typical example. The other data in the form – such as login or account creation details – will only be accepted by the application if the characters are copied correctly.

Implementing a simple image CAPTCHA is quite easy if your Web application can make use of a suitable graphics library, such as **Image Magick**. All you need to do is generate a random string of characters of a suitable length, then pass it to the library to render as a bitmapped image to which you apply some distortion and add a noisy background. The text string is stored so that it can be compared with the text entered in the box. Plug-ins are available for adding CAPTCHAs that work in this way to applications built with most of the common server-side technologies. You should be aware, though, that basic image CAPTCHAs obviously present serious accessibility problems (as we discuss shortly) for which reason they should usually be avoided.

Type the code shown [   ]   ↻ Try a new code

Figure 5. *A typical CAPTCHA*

From a technical point of view, CAPTCHAs were reasonably successful when they were first introduced, but more sophisticated OCR techniques soon allowed spammers to solve CAPTCHAs based on simple distortion of rendered text. Because the distortion is applied algorithmically, it can be removed algorithmically. A sort of arms race has developed between the spammers and the people who devise CAPTCHA algorithms. As the CAPTCHAs get harder, more sophisticated techniques are developed for breaking them. The result is that CAPTCHAs are becoming steadily harder for legitimate users to decipher, even if their eyesight is good.

For the many users who do not have good vision, however, even the less distorted image CAPTCHAs are inaccessible. Screen readers cannot interpret the images, as CAPTCHA images are deliberately devised to prevent machine-reading, but alt attributes cannot be provided to assist visually impaired users in the usual way. Using alt attributes would defeat the purpose of CAPTCHAs, since the alt text could be read by any program, not just by screen readers. The reCAPTCHA alternative, described below, always provides an audio alternative for anyone who cannot see the images or who finds them difficult to interpret, so it is more accessible, if not necessarily more usable.

The *reCAPTCHA* project takes an interesting approach to generating CAPTCHAs in conjunction with the effort to digitize old newspapers and books. Instead of creating CAPTCHAs from randomly generated characters, reCAPTCHA uses real words from scanned documents which two different OCR programs have failed to process successfully. Through the reCAPTCHA project, a database has been built up which

Figure 6. *An example from the reCAPTCHA project (left) and a reCAPTCHA in use on a user account login page (right)*

includes both the images of words which have yet to be deciphered and images of words which have now been identified. Web site owners may use the reCAPTCHA API to send for pairs of these word images to use on pages where it's important to prevent programs from submitting forms or content. (Inevitably, you must create an account with ReCaptcha before you can do this.) In each pair of word images, one image represents a word that has been identified, which functions as the actual CAPTCHA, while the other image shows a word that has not yet been identified. Some distortion is applied to both images to make them harder for OCR software to recognize. Users must type both the words that these images represent into a box on the form to be submitted, as shown in Figure 6.

In addition to allowing the user to proceed (if they enter the known CAPTCHA word correctly), both the words entered in the reCAPTCHA box are passed back to the reCAPTCHA project for processing there. It is assumed that if the user has managed to interpret the known CAPTCHA word image accurately then they have probably interpreted the other image correctly too. When enough users have both solved a CAPTCHA and provided the same answer for a previously unidentified word image, the word in that image is assumed to have been identified correctly. It is then added to the digitized version of the document from which it was taken, as well as to the collection of known words used to generate reCAPTCHAs. By asking users to identify two words, the project helps to prevent the creation of phoney accounts and other robot activity, adds to the stock of potential CAPTCHAs, and furthers the digitization of old texts.

Another solution to the inaccessibility of image CAPTCHAs is to dispense with images altogether and ask randomly generated simple questions, such as "What is the sum of 5 + 2?" instead. Mathematical questions can be asked and answered precisely, so they are a good choice for this purpose, though it is necessary to keep them simple. ("What do you get if you integrate cosh $5x$ with respect to x?" is probably not a good CAPTCHA for most sites, for example.) Using arithmetic problems also ensures that questions are not culturally dependent, such as the question "What is the fifth letter of the alphabet?", where the answer is contingent on the user's language. Programs can easily be developed to parse questions that pose simple arithmetic problems, though, so this type of CAPTCHA is vulnerable to automatic cracking, especially as it becomes more widespread and the forms of question become well known.

There are two other drawbacks to using any kind of CAPTCHA. First, they can always be solved by people. Sufficiently well organized gangs can make use of large numbers of people to solve CAPTCHAs by offering employment in parts of the world where labour is cheap and work is badly needed. It is only necessary to relay a word image to a "CAPTCHA-cracking factory", or perhaps just send it to someone's mobile phone, in order to get the answer back. This process makes signing up slower than a fully automatic script, but allows determined spammers to create accounts on thousands of sites.

The last drawback of CAPTCHAs is perhaps the most intractable. Just about everybody hates them. Of course they do. Being asked to squint at some barely legible text, decipher it, then type it into a form, all before you can create an account just to answer a question on a forum or upload a photo of your cat (for example) is an indefensible imposition. Like many security precautions, the effect is to treat the vast majority of users, who have only good intentions, as potential criminals or vandals. Apart from being insulting, such behaviour is likely to deter desirable users and customers, especially if the CAPTCHAs used are hard to decipher correctly. How many people will persist in the face of their repeated failure to copy some distorted characters, just so that they can create an account on your site?

A different approach to foiling attempts to create accounts by programs is to force the program to do something that a person would not do, instead of forcing a person to do something that a program could not do. It seems to be the case that many programs for creating accounts automatically will enter text into every text field on a form, on the assumption that every field may be compulsory. If a text field is added to a form, but hidden using CSS so that people never see it, there will be a high probability that if data for that field is included in the request which is sent when the form is submitted, the form was submitted by a program, not a person. In that case, instead of creating an account (or carrying out any other request which the form was being used for), the application should redirect to a special page. It is possible that screen readers may still see the text field although it is hidden from sight, so it should be labelled "Do not type in this field". It's also conceivable that somebody might disable CSS and enter text in such a field anyway, so – just in case a legitimate user does manage to enter text in the hidden field – the special page they are redirected to ought to provide an explanation of what has happened and why. Anecdotal evidence suggests that "negative CAPTCHAs" of this kind can be effective, although we are not aware of any firm quantitative evidence for this.

The unpopularity of CAPTCHAs and their accessibility problems mean that they should only be used judiciously, if at all (notwithstanding the fact that most social networking sites and other major Web service providers continue to use CAPTCHAs at the time of writing). Since CAPTCHAs and reCAPTCHAs can be added to an application very easily, it is advisable to omit them when an application is first launched, and only use them later if it becomes clear that accounts created by programs are becoming a serious problem. It may be worth trying a negative CAPTCHA first. If you decide to use a CAPTCHA when a user creates an account, it should not be necessary to use one every time a user logs in. In any case, the effectiveness of any scheme should be monitored.

If automatic account creation becomes a major nuisance on your site, you can require users to reply to a confirmatory email sent to the address they provide when creating an account. (Programs usually give false addresses.)

Again, this is annoying for legitimate users and may put some off, but there comes a point when spam renders a site useless, so that spammers have to be prevented from creating accounts. There are ways of filtering spam, of course, which should routinely be applied to any user-generated content, but that topic lies beyond the scope of this book.

Resetting Passwords

People quite often forget the password associated with their user account. When this happens, there is a problem. If passwords are the sole means of authentication, the password is all that the application can rely on to distinguish between someone whose email address really is, for example, abe@abelardos.com.fd, and someone else who claims that that is their email address. If the genuine Abelardo has forgotten his password, the application can no longer distinguish him from any fake Abelardos. Thus, a request claiming to be from Abelardo, asking to be given a new password or otherwise allowed to log in again without entering the password, could have come from anybody.

Some Web sites ask users for additional "security information" when they create accounts, such as the name of their first school, or their place of birth. When the user forgets their password they are asked for some or all of this information. If they provide correct answers to these "security questions" they are allowed to log in and set a new password. This is not a secure practice. (It is also worth observing that these questions are often culturally insensitive, especially the common question "What is your mother's maiden name?" In some cultures, this question has little meaning as women do not change their names on marriage; in others, a person's full name includes their mother's maiden name, and so on.)

Hackers can find the answers to standard security questions for individual users surprisingly easily in many cases. If they are able to determine a piece of information such as someone's place of birth once, they can use it again wherever it has been left as security information. The user can always lie about the answers to these questions, of course, but most people don't, and if they do it carries the risk of their forgetting the fictitious answer. The same risk applies when a site allows the user to set both the question and the answer. Ultimately, it is possible that somebody will forget all the security information they provided as well as their password, so – whatever precautions you try to adopt – you will eventually need some mechanism for resetting passwords.

The only assumption that can be made with reasonable confidence is that email messages sent to the address stored in the database for a particular user's account will only be read by that user. (Even that is not necessarily true, but it has to be assumed.) The simplest solution from the user's immediate point of view might be to have their plaintext password sent to them by email, but the risks of having plaintext passwords exposed should always outweigh any other considerations. As we stressed earlier, you should never store users' passwords in unencrypted form or use a reversible algorithm to encrypt them. It follows that a secure Web application is not able to send a user their current password under any circumstances.

The easiest alternative is for the Web application to provide a temporary new password. The login form should include a link labelled something like "Forgotten your password?", which points to a form with just a single field for the email address and a submit button labelled "Get New Password". When this form is submitted, the email address is looked up to confirm that it is associated with an existing account. If it is, a random string is generated, and assigned to that account's password. An email message containing this new temporary password is then sent to the address provided in the form. It is prudent to restrict the use of the generated password to a single login, and to require it to be changed immediately the user has logged in.

This scheme is simple to implement, but has a weakness in that it allows anyone who knows someone else's email address to request that their password be reset. As email addresses are often quite widely known or easily discovered, a practical joker can cause a nuisance in this way. It is also possible that a rudimentary denial of service attack could be mounted by repeatedly sending requests to change users' passwords.

To avoid these problems, a more elaborate password reset method can be adopted. When a Web application receives a request claiming that the password for an account has been forgotten, and has confirmed that the email address is associated with a user account, the password is not reset by the application, but a unique random string, usually called a *reset token*, is generated and stored in the user's account record. A message is then sent to the user's email address. This message contains a URL that incorporates the same random string (that is, the reset token), for example,

```
http://www.abelardos.com.fd/password_reset/01229d671571
```

The message should also include some text, informing the user that a password reset request has been received, and assuring them that their account has not been compromised. It should let them know that if they did not submit the request themselves they can safely ignore the message and their password will not be changed.

If the request was legitimate, and the user clicks on the link provided (or enters the URL in their browser's address bar, if they are cautious), they will see a form with a field to confirm their email address and other fields in which to enter and confirm a new password. On submission of this form the password will be changed so that they can log in again.

A field called password_reset_token must be added to the users table, to hold the value of the reset token generated in response to a password reset request. Some minor additions are needed to the User model to accommodate the extra piece of data. The major extensions are shown in Listing 6. They consist of a trivial method to find a User object given a reset token (shown on lines 11–13), and a property, which generates and clears tokens. Since the value and structure of the token should not affect anything outside the model, the setter for this property takes a Boolean argument indicating whether to set or clear the token. If this argument is true, a fairly short random string, hex-encoded to ensure that it can be embedded in a URL, is generated on line 7, using a method implemented in the rbytes module, which is a wrapper around *OpenSSL*'s cryptographically secure

Listing 6

```
1   Object.defineProperty(User.prototype, 'resetToken', {
2     get: function(attribute){
3       return this._passwordResetToken;
4     },
5     set: function(t) {
6       this._passwordResetToken =
7               t? rbytes.randomBytes(6).toHex():'';
8     }
9   });
10
11  User.findByPasswordResetToken = function(e, callback) {
12    User.find('password_reset_token', e, callback);
13  };
```

random number generator. The new _passwordResetToken property must be added to User.persistentProperties so that the value will be saved to the database.

A controller module that implements the operations needed by this password resetting scheme is provided in Listing 7. The controller actions are called in response to requests according to the following route definitions (see the *Introduction*):

```
app.get('/password_reset/request', passwordResetController.new);
app.post('/password_reset', passwordResetController.create);
app.get('/password_reset/:token', passwordResetController.edit);
app.put('/password_reset', passwordResetController.update);
```

The new action method is invoked when a request is sent with the path /password_reset/request. The link on which a user should click if they have forgotten their password will have a URL containing this path as the value of its href attribute. The new action just renders a simple form requesting an email address. When this is submitted using a POST request to /password_reset the create action is called. This extracts the email address from the request body and tries to look up a corresponding User object. If the lookup is successful, a token is generated, by assigning true

Listing 7

```
 1  module.exports = function(User) {
 2
 3      var send_reset_message = require('../lib/reset').send_
reset_message;
 4
 5    return {
 6     new: function(req, res){
 7      res.render('password_resets/new',
 8                  { title : 'Request Password Reset',
 9                    u: null});
10     },
11
12     create: function(req, res){
13      var address = req.body.user.email;
14      User.findByEmail(address, function(err, theUser) {
15        if (theUser && !err) {
16         theUser.resetToken = true;
17         theUser.save(function(err) {
18          if (err) {
19           req.flash('error', err.message);
20           res.render('password_resets/new',
21                       { title : 'Request Password Reset',
22                         u: theUser});
23          }
24          else
25           send_reset_message(theUser, res);
26         })
27
28        }
29        else {
30         req.flash('error',
31           'There is no account with email address ' + address);
32         res.render('password_resets/new',
33                     { title : 'Request Password Reset',
34                       u: null});
35        }
36      });
37     },
```

```
38   edit: function(req, res){
39    User.findByPasswordResetToken(req.params.token,
40      function(err, theUser) {
41       if (theUser && !err)
42         res.render('password_resets/edit',
43                    {title: 'Reset Password', u: theUser});
44       else
45         res.redirect('password_resets/new', 404);
46      });
47   },
48
49   update: function(req, res){
50    var userData = req.body.user;
51    User.findByEmail(userData.email, function(err, theUser) {
52     var badUpdate = function(message) {
53      req.flash('error', message);
54      res.render('password_resets/edit',
55                 {title: 'Reset Password', u: theUser});
56     };
57
58     if (theUser && !err &&
59       theUser.resetToken == userData.reset_token &&
60       userData.password == userData.confirm) {
61      theUser.resetToken = false;
62      theUser.password = userData.password;
63      theUser.save(function(err) {
64       if (err)
65        badUpdate(err.message);
66       else
67        res.render('password_resets/updated',
68                   {title: 'Password successfully reset'});
69      });
70     }
71     else
72      badUpdate('could not reset the password, bad data');
73    });
74   }
75  }
76 }
```

to the `resetToken` property of the `User` object returned. The object, complete with token, is then saved. If all goes well, the `send_token` method (whose definition we will not show, as the details of sending emails are not relevant) sends an email message containing a URL, such as the one displayed earlier, which is generated from the token. Otherwise, or if the lookup failed, the form is displayed to the user again, with a suitable notice.

If the user who receives the email message clicks on the link it contains, they will invoke the `edit` action, and `req.params.token` will be set to the unique token in the email message. This value is used to find the corresponding `User` record. If the lookup fails, either the token is corrupt or a break-in attempt is being made, so the original request form is displayed again. If the lookup succeeds, it is assumed that the request came from the person who received the email message, who ought to be the owner of the account. In that case, a form is displayed for them to enter a new password. In contrast to the situation in which a user chooses to change their password, it is not possible to require the user to enter the old password – the reason for going through this current procedure is that they have forgotten the old password. Instead, the reset token is embedded in the form in a hidden field, and checked against the stored token for the user when the form is submitted and the `update` action is executed. If this was omitted, it would be possible for an attacker to synthesize a request to the `update` action without knowing the token, and thus to change the password. If the token check succeeds, the password record is updated and the user can log in.

The token should be deleted after the password has been changed, as it is at line 61 of Listing 7, in case somebody gets hold of the URL later. For additional security, the token should also be deleted after a short time if it is not used, so that there is only a limited opportunity for the password to be changed.

Key Points

- It is advisable to require confirmation of the password when a user first creates an account.

- The value typed in an HTML input element whose type attribute is set to password is masked – that is, the characters entered by the user are displayed as a row of bullets or asterisks.

- Some user interface experts dislike the use of masked password fields, on the grounds that they offer little security but prevent valuable interface feedback for the user.

- It is vital to ensure, so far as you can, that nobody is able to change a user's password except the user whose password it is.

- Confirmation of the password should be required before a user can edit or delete their account.

- Submitting forms to create or update an account means sending a user's email address and password over the network. Both the form and the submitted data should ideally be sent over HTTPS.

- If you want to embed a small login form on every page, you should consider serving the entire site over HTTPS.

- It is essential to make sure that passwords are never recorded in log files. Passwords and their confirmations should always be excluded from logging.

- Spammers and other hackers have developed programs that can traverse the Web automatically, creating accounts wherever they find the opportunity.

- CAPTCHAs were designed to prevent user accounts from being created automatically by programs.

- Simple CAPTCHAs require a user to recognize distorted text presented as an image. While this is possible for many humans, it defeats programs if the text is sufficiently distorted.

- The reCAPTCHA project provides images of words from scanned documents which OCR software failed to interpret correctly. When these words are recognized by users during account creation or login procedures, the results are passed back to the project to help digitize old documents.

- Conventional CAPTCHAs present serious accessibility problems. Some CAPTCHAs and all reCAPTCHAs offer an audio alternative for people who cannot read the images.

- Simple mathematical puzzles may be used instead of images, but these are probably more easily defeated by programs.

- CAPTCHAs are deservedly unpopular and should only be used judiciously if at all.

- A different approach to preventing programs from creating accounts is to force the program to do something that a person would not do, instead of vice versa.

- A text field on a form can be hidden from human view using CSS. If data for that field is included when the form is submitted, there is a high probability that it has been entered by a program.

- If automatic account creation becomes a major nuisance, you may have to use email confirmations and spam filtering.

- If a user forgets their password, the primary means of verifying their identity is lost.

- Careful precautions must be taken to prevent abuse of any facility for resetting lost passwords.

- Relying on "additional security information" – such as place of birth – to confirm identity is unsafe, as this information is often readily discovered.

- Security questions may also be culturally insensitive, especially the common question "What is your mother's maiden name?" Such questions should be avoided.

- It is necessary to assume that messages sent to the email address stored for a user will only be read by that user.

- An application can reset a password to a random value and then email it to the user, but this is open to abuse by practical jokers who may request password resets for other users.

- An application can email a special token to the user, which is then used to verify their identity before allowing them to reset their password.

Authentication

It's tempting to suppose that logging in to a Web site, or "signing in" as it's sometimes called, is similar to what might happen if you were visiting a large company's offices for a meeting. In that case, you might literally sign in – that is, you would sign your name on a sheet to record the fact that you were in the building. When you left, you would sign out to record your departure. You would only be considered to have a right to be in the building during the period between signing in and signing out. Logging in to a Web site may seem to be like that, inasmuch as you are only considered to have a right to access restricted resources on that site between logging in and logging out. Where the doorman demands your signature before you can enter a company's offices, a Web application normally asks for your password. This requires that you have an account, but apart from that it is used in a similar way to your signature, as a means of authenticating your identity.

This analogy is misleading, however. HTTP is a stateless protocol. The server deals with each request in isolation and retains no state from previous requests. This means that there is no sense in which a user can be "allowed in" to the application, in the way you can be allowed in to an office building when you sign in. Logging in to a Web site is more like obtaining a swipe-card that will let you in to the building every time you come back. Logging out means surrendering the card. The analogy is strained, though, because you need to imagine that this building is one in which you can only do one thing before you have to leave. If you need to do something else, you must return, using your card to get back in again.

Most commonly, the equivalent of the swipe card in this analogy is an HTTP *cookie*. When you log in to a Web site, the server sends a cookie to your browser. Every time you send a request to that site, your browser sends the cookie back with the request headers. The Web site's code on the server end must use the cookie to associate the request with your account. If there is no cookie in the request, if the cookie has been corrupted, or if the cookie cannot be associated with a logged-in user's account, the application will deny access to restricted resources.

Session-Based Authentication

The need to remember whether a user is logged in is a specific case of a problem characteristic of many Web applications – that is, the need to remember state information between requests. As we have just remarked, HTTP is a stateless protocol and, for efficiency reasons, the server deals with each request in isolation. Once it has sent a response, it deletes all information pertaining to the request. If another request is subsequently sent by the same user, the server has no way of associating it with the earlier request. However, applications frequently need to maintain information about a particular user's interactions with them. For example, e-commerce applications usually maintain a shopping basket or cart. A customer can add several items to the basket before checking out and paying for them all at once. Many requests may be made between the time the first item is added to the basket and the time payment is made. The items must be remembered between requests and, when a request is received, the appropriate basket must be retrieved. The HTTP protocol provides no way of doing this, so some other mechanism must be employed.

Some representation of the state of the interaction between the user and application must be sent back in the response, stored in the user's browser and then sent to the server with the next request and passed on to the application. There are three places where this information may be carried: the response body, the request data (including any query string), and the message headers. One fairly popular technique is to include some data in the response body, in the form of hidden input fields, which will be returned in the query string or POST data of the response. As you can deduce, this method will only work when the interaction makes use of HTML forms for each request. A more generally useful technique is to embed the state information in query strings for GET requests, modifying any links appropriately when the page is generated. For example, a link pointing to a checkout page may include a string identifying a user's basket, like this:

```
<a href="checkout.php?basket_id=BX199">proceed to checkout</a>
```

In this scheme, the state information is included in the response body in the form of links with query strings that depend on the state. This state information is sent back to the server in the query string when a link is clicked. We shall explain later why this may not be a secure way of preserving state.

The most popular option for preserving state makes use of message headers for transporting the state information between the client and server. When this is done, the state takes the form of a small piece of data called a *cookie*.

Cookies

Cookies are not defined as part of the purely stateless HTTP protocol, but are an extension defined in a separate standard. Nevertheless, they are supported by all mainstream browsers and HTTP servers, and are an essential component of many Web applications. It is possible for browser users to disable cookies or restrict the domains from which they are accepted, but there are now so many sites that depend on cookies for their functioning that it is not unreasonable to take the view that users who choose to reject cookies have deliberately denied themselves the use of your Web application, so you should not worry about providing any special workarounds for their benefit.

Cookies are exchanged between browsers and servers by way of two headers provided for the purpose, Set-Cookie and Cookie. The first step in an interaction using cookies comes when the server sends a Set-Cookie header to the browser – it is always the server that starts off cookie exchanges. Normally, once a browser has accepted a cookie it will send it back unchanged in every request to the same domain, until the cookie expires and is no longer considered valid.

A Set-Cookie header consists of several parts, separated by semi-colons. For instance,

```
Set-Cookie: exp_last_activity=1265066352; expires=Tue, 01-Feb-
2014 18:19:12 GMT; path=/
```

This site is setting a cookie with the name exp_last_activity. Each part of the header consists of a name, an = sign, and a value, which is a string. Some names are defined in the cookie standard with specific meanings; these are called *attributes*. The first name in a header is treated as the cookie's name, and the value is the string that gets stored in the browser under that name. As you can see in this example, the cookie values are often encoded in some way, so although it is easy to guess what exp_last_activity means, it is far from obvious what the value is.

The remaining names set values for attributes. The expires attribute specifies the time and date until which the cookie may be used. If this value is not provided, the cookie expires at the end of the browsing session, that is, when the user quits the browser. As you probably know, it is possible for a user to delete cookies from their browser at any time, so there can be no guarantee that a cookie will persist until the time set for it to expire.

The final attribute is the path. The cookie will be returned by the browser in any request for a page on the site within the directory specified by the path. In our example, the cookies will be sent with every request to that site, since the path is /, indicating the site root.

A Set-Cookie header may include a few other attributes, of which the most significant is domain. As its name suggests, this attribute can be used to set the domain name to which the cookie applies.

Unless the domain attribute is present in the header, the cookie will be sent with any requests to the domain that issued it, or to any sub-domains of that domain. For instance, if a Set-Cookie header was sent in a response from the domain abelardos.com.fd, and the path attribute was set to /, the cookies it contained would be returned in all requests sent to abelardos.com.fd, but also to www.abelardos.com.fd, store.abelardos.com.fd, and support.abelardos.com.fd, if those sub-domains existed.

If the domain attribute is present, it can be used to expand the set of domains to which the cookies are sent, as well as restrict it. Suppose, for instance, you sent a request to www.abelardos.com.fd. In that case, any cookie that was set in the response would only be returned to that domain and any sub-domains it may have, but not to store.abelardos.com.fd, for example, as this is not a sub-domain of www.abelardos.com.fd. By setting the domain attribute to a prefix of the domain name, such as .abelardos.com.fd, the cookie could be used by the entire domain.

If there were no restrictions on the domains that could be specified, this would allow cookies to be used for tracking users' Web browsing habits, and perhaps for other undesirable purposes too. Therefore, the domain attribute's value can only be the domain from which the response is being sent, or a prefix of that domain name (in which case the attribute's value conventionally begins with a .). This restriction is the *same-origin policy* for cookies. Most browsers will ignore cookies if only the highest-level domains (the ones that you cannot register) are specified. That is, a domain attribute's value may not be .com or .co.uk and so on. The rules used by each country for the structure of URLs for which they are responsible are not consistent, so for some domains this restriction is not correctly implemented in all browsers.

Two other attributes relevant to security are Secure and HttpOnly. These two attributes do not have a value, they are simply present or absent. The former specifies that the cookie should only be sent over a secure connection. That is, it can only be used with HTTPS, which will mean that it is always encrypted, so the risk of it being hijacked is reduced. If the Secure attribute is not set, any request using HTTP will include the cookie. On sites that mix HTTPS and HTTP (for instance, using HTTP to fetch images), setting the attribute will ensure that unencrypted cookies are not sent inadvertently.

If HttpOnly is specified, the cookie will not be exposed to client-side scripts. This restriction reduces the potential mischief that may be caused by *cross-site scripting*.

When a request is sent to a page within a domain for which the browser has a cookie that has not yet expired, the cookies are returned in the Cookie header, unless the Secure attribute is set and the protocol is not HTTPS. Only the cookie names and their values are returned. The attributes that may have been included in the Set-Cookie header are not returned. Hence, if a request was sent to the site that sent the example Set-Cookie header shown above, it would include the following header:

```
Cookie: exp_last_activity=1265072193
```

Although requests and responses are sent to and from the actual Web server, cookies may be set and read by any application that communicates with the server, so in effect these values are passed between the application and the user's browser. On the client side, cookies without the HttpOnly attribute may be read or written by way of the document.cookie object in JavaScript.

You can probably see that an application which maintains user accounts could set the value of a cookie called user to a user's id when they log in. If the same user sends further requests during the same browsing session, the value from the cookie can be used to look up their account. If there is no cookie or the lookup fails, the request did not come from a logged-in user, so access to any restricted pages will be denied.

Hopefully, you can also see that such a scheme is too simple-minded. Cookies' values are plain text strings. Tools that allow you to see the value of response headers and modify the values in request headers are readily available. Since user ids are typically sequential numbers, it would be trivial to set the user cookie's value in a request to some number other than your own id. A few attempts would probably allow you to become logged in as some other user and access their account. Clearly, a more elaborate scheme for remembering users by means of cookies is required.

Sessions

Cookies are not just useful for maintaining logins. They can be used for a myriad of purposes, including shopping baskets, user preferences and analytics. But writing and parsing HTTP headers is a repetitive and low-level way of dealing with state information. A higher-level abstraction is normally available in server-side scripting languages and frameworks, in the form of *sessions*. In this context a session is just an object or some other associative data structure, which appears to persist between requests from the same source. Thus, to remember a value for a user's id, you would simply store it in the session.

For example, in Express the session is an object, which is in turn a property of the `request` object. In a controller method to which the request is passed as an argument called `req`, the `id` of a `User` record called `theUser` could be stored in the session by the assignment:

```
req.session.userId = theUser.id;
```

Later, you could retrieve the user id from a `request` object in the variable `req` just by using the expression `req.session.userId`. You can do the same thing in Ruby on Rails with the `session` instance method of the `ActionController` class, in PHP with the `$_SESSION` array, or in Django with `request.session`, using the appropriate Ruby, PHP or Python constructs respectively, for storing and retrieving the values.

Cookies are used to keep track of sessions, but there are several ways in which this may be done. A naive approach is to map each element of the session to a separate cookie, with the cookie name being available as a key in the session hash. Using this scheme, the user's id, `req.session.userId`, would be transmitted back and forth between the server and browser in a cookie whose name was `userId`, and so on.

The data in cookies is visible to anybody who can obtain the cookie, legitimately or otherwise, so you should not allow any critical data (such as personal details or credit card numbers) to be included in a session that was implemented directly as a collection of cookies. If confidential data is included in a cookie, it should be encrypted. If HTTPS is being used, cookies will be encrypted during transit. This will prevent their being intercepted, but they will be decrypted and readable in the browser. As we will explain later, allowing users to see the contents of cookies may be a security risk, even when the data pertains to the user's own account, so it will be necessary to encrypt the session data in the application. This will ensure that the cookie cannot be read when it is stored in a browser, and it also removes the need to use HTTPS to hide its contents in transit. Notice that since the encryption and decryption are only ever performed in the Web application code, there is no need to exchange any keys, so the characteristic problem of shared key encryption does not occur.

Unencrypted cookie data can not only be read, it can also be changed easily. To prevent tampering with the session data, it is possible to add a **MAC (Message Authentication Code)** – a cryptographic hash of the cookie's contents which can only be computed using a secret key – so that any interference can be detected. When this is done, it is normal to combine the elements of the session into a single cookie. Typically, the session object is serialized as **JSON**, YAML or some similar data interchange format, and the **HMAC** (a MAC computed using a standard construction) of the string is computed, with the key being a secret that is generated when the application is deployed.

Even if a MAC is added or the cookie is protected by encryption, it is quite possible that a user could destroy their session data, since they can delete cookies at any time.

The main advantage of cookie-based session storage is that it is efficient, compared with the alternatives. There is no need to access a database or a file to retrieve the session data, as it's all there in the HTTP request.

Storing sessions in cookies may be the most efficient option for small amounts of data, but it has several limitations. Some browsers – most importantly, older versions of Internet Explorer – impose a limit on the size

> ### Session Cookies
>
> The phrase "session cookie" is used to mean a cookie that persists for the duration of a single browsing session, that is, it is kept in the browser's cookie store until the user quits the program, which could be anything from a few moments to several months later. The usage may be confusing: a session cookie is not necessarily being used to store a session id, while a cookie that is used to store a session id is not necessarily a session cookie and may have an explicit expiry time.

and number of cookies they will store. In practice, it is safest to assume that the maximum length of cookie that can be stored is 4 kB. This is evidently enough for a user id, but it may not be enough for more complex data.

A more flexible way of preserving session data is to use a database. Almost all Web applications store information in a database anyway, so in most cases this will not require much additional work. In a relational database, a special sessions table is created, which has at least two columns: session_id and data. (The precise names are arbitrary.) The session_id column holds a specially generated key for each session. This key needs to be unique, unpredictable and ideally opaque – that is, somebody looking at its value would be unable to determine how it was constructed. In Express, session ids are created by concatenating a 24-byte pseudo-random string and a dot with the base 64-encoded HMAC of the same string prefixed to the user agent string contained in the most recent HTTP request. The HMAC is keyed by a secret generated for the application, and uses SHA-256 as the hash function. It is thus effectively random, although the actual amount of entropy in the computation is relatively low, leaving the id somewhat vulnerable to attacks if the key were to become known.

The data column holds a serialized version of the session hash, that is, some string representation such as JSON from which the hash object can be reconstructed when it is retrieved from the database. Looking up the session for a given session id can be made efficient by creating an index on the session_id column of the sessions table.

If the actual session data is available in a database table as described, all that needs to be sent back and forth in a cookie is the session id. The base 64 version of an SHA-256 hash is 43 bytes long, so the complete session id computed by Express is 68 bytes long, which can easily fit within the limit for the size of an individual cookie. The cookie's name is arbitrary. Express uses connect.sid by default, but variations on names like sessionid are common in applications built on other frameworks.

The use of a database to store session data is not restricted to relational databases. If a NoSQL database is being used to store an application's persistent data, it can be used to store session data as well. The same general scheme is used, with a session identifier being sent in a cookie. The only difference lies in the way the identifier is used to retrieve the associated data. If a suitable abstraction layer is being used on top of the database the difference would be insignificant, as an object would be retrieved by an appropriate method call taking the session id value as its argument.

If there is a reason not to store the session in a database, there are still some alternatives to putting the session data into the cookie itself. The hash can be serialized and written to a temporary file – the session id can be used as the file name, making it simple to retrieve the data once the id has been read from the Cookie header in a request. However, reading from and writing to files on disk is normally much slower than retrieving and updating records in a database, so this option is unsuitable for heavily used applications.

If simplicity and high speed are desired, another option is to store the session data in memory. A globally accessible sessions object is created by the application framework, and sessions are stored in it. This technique cannot be considered suitable for most production environments. It can only work if the application server is running as a single process, so it will not scale to multiple servers. Also, orphaned sessions will continue to consume memory. Finally, if the application should crash or be restarted for any reason, all sessions will be lost. Storing sessions in memory is usually best reserved for prototype applications (but it is the default session storage mechanism in Express).

At the opposite extreme, heavily-used Web applications that need to handle millions of requests every day, and which may be distributed over many servers, often cache all their frequently-accessed data. Sessions can usefully be included in the cache. A popular option for caching in distributed applications is memcached, a high-performance, distributed object caching system. Sessions stored using memcached are still accessed by way of a session id, which is exchanged with the client in a cookie.

As you will gather from these examples of session storage, all methods that do not store the entire session in a cookie rely on exchanging a session id between the client and server in a cookie. They therefore all share the same vulnerabilities associated with cookies, as we will describe shortly.

Authentication Using Sessions

An authentication method must provide a mechanism for logging users in, checking their credentials in the process, and a way of restricting access to a site, or parts of it, to only those users who have successfully logged in. An explicit means of logging out is also generally to be preferred. How can sessions be used to provide these facilities?

We'll begin by considering the login process for authentication that is based on sessions. There must be a page that displays a form, with text fields for email address (or user name) and password. Listing 8 shows a minimal **EJS** template for such a form. With suitable CSS, it can readily be styled to match the forms displayed in the previous chapter. Notice the links for creating an account and resetting a forgotten password. These point to the pages we described in that chapter.

This template will be rendered when a user first attempts to log in, and it may need to be rendered again if the login attempt fails. In that case, it is considerate to populate the email field with the address that was entered the first time. When this happens, we will arrange that a User object is passed as a local variable called u. The method maybe used on line 11 is a trivial convenience method that helps us avoid problems if u is undefined.

Listing 8

```
1  <h1>Log In</h1>
2  <p>You must log in using a recognized email address and valid
password to use this site.</p>
3  <p>If you do not have an account, you can
<a href="/user/new">create one</a> easily and quickly. We only
need your email address and a password, we don't ask for any other
personal information.</p>
4
5  <div id="log-in-form">
6    <%- messages() %>
7    <form action="/login" method="post">
8    <div class="field required">
9     <label for="user_email">Your email address</label>
10     <input type="text" name="user[email]" id="user_email"
11         value="<%- maybe(u, 'email') %>"/>
12    </div>
13    <div class="field required">
14     <label for="user_password">Your password</label>
15     <input type="password" name="user[password]"
16         id="user_password" />
17    </div>
18
19    <p class="hint">
20      <a href="/password_reset/request">Have you forgotten your
password?</a>
21    </p>
22    <input type="submit" name="submit" value="Log in"
id="submit" />
23    </form>
24  </div>
```

We add maybe as a helper method in the application's main program, which
makes it available in all views:

```
app.helpers({
  maybe: function(obj, prop) { return obj? obj[prop]: ''; }
});
```

If the form is re-rendered, we will also want to display a helpful message, telling the user what went wrong. The messages module offers a means of passing messages between requests. On line 6 of Listing 8 we use the messages method to display any message which may have been constructed in the controller.

Notice that, as we mentioned in connection with the account creation form in the previous chapter, the name attribute of the input element for the email address is set to user[email], and the name attribute of the input element for the password is set to user[password] (lines 10 and 15 of Listing 8). Because the elements are named in this way, Express will arrange for an object called user, with properties email and password containing the values entered into the input elements, to be included in the object containing the request body, so our controller will be able to extract them easily.

Most of the controller, shown in Listing 9, is trivial. It treats a "login" as a singular resource which cannot be edited, so the only operations that need to be defined are new and create, for displaying the login page and performing authentication, and destroy, for logging out. (A more accurate name for this resource would be loginSession, but the word "session" is already burdened with too many meanings.) As in other examples, we have shown the HTTP requests that invoke these actions as comments above each method definition.

The only method in Listing 9 that requires comment is create, defined on lines 18–29. Its body consists entirely of a call to the static method checkCredentials, which we defined in the User model in the last chapter. The email and password arguments are taken from the request body's user property, which will have been set up when the form was submitted, as we described above.

Remember that checkCredentials takes a callback as its third argument, and this callback's first argument is null if the credentials were valid and no errors occurred, or an Error object otherwise. The callback can check

Listing 9

```
 1  module.exports = function(User) {
 2  var loginUser = function(req, res, theUser) {
 3      req.session.userId = theUser.id;
 4      if (req.session.requestedUrl)
 5        res.redirect(req.session.requestedUrl)
 6      else
 7        res.redirect('/user');
 8  };
 9
10   return {
11    // GET /login
12    new: function(req, res) {
13     res.render('logins/new',
14          {title: 'Login', u: null, layout: 'blank-layout'})
15    },
16
17    // POST /login
18    create: function(req, res) {
19     User.checkCredentials(req.body.user.email,
20      req.body.user.password, function(err, theUser) {
21       if (!err)
22         loginUser(req, res, theUser);
23       else {
24         req.flash('error', err.message);
25         res.render('logins/new',
26              {title: 'Login', u: theUser});
27       }
28     });
29    },
30
31    // DELETE /logout
32    destroy: function(req, res) {
33      req.session.destroy(function(err) {
34       res.render('logins/farewell',
35                {title: 'Logged Out', layout: 'blank-layout'});
36      });
37    }
38  }
39 }
```

this value (line 21) and if it is null, call the function loginUser to store the id value of the User object it has been passed in the session, using the assignment on line 3. If the credentials were not valid, the user is shown the login page again, by the render on line 25. The call on the line above to flash, a method defined in the messages module, sets the message to be displayed on the page, telling the user what has happened. If a User object is passed to the callback, it will be passed into the template as the local variable u, so that a valid email address will be re-displayed, as required.

A question remains. What page should a user be redirected to after they have successfully logged in? There are two cases to consider. Either they tried to access a restricted resource, and were redirected to the login page (in a way we will describe shortly), or they explicitly clicked on a Log In link. In the first case, we are going to arrange for the URL they requested to be remembered in the session while they log in. It will be the value of req.session.requestedUrl, so on line 4 we check whether this has a value. If it does, we use it as the destination of a redirect. If not, the user must have clicked on a Log In link, so we redirect them to a welcome page.

A logout action is also needed. This just destroys the session on line 33 of Listing 9 and renders a leaving page.

Don't forget that with a scheme such as the one just described for logging in, users' credentials are sent to the server in plaintext form. To prevent any possibility of eavesdropping, the login therefore needs to be performed over a secure channel, using HTTPS.

To make this scheme work, we need to be able to call a method when a request is received, before the controller method to deal with the request is invoked. Express provides a convenient means of doing just that. As we mentioned in the *Introduction*, "middleware" may be specified when the routes are defined for an Express application. The middleware for each route comprises methods that should be called before the controller method for that route. For authorization, we need to place a method that we will call restrictToAuthenticated in front of any action for a restricted URL.

For instance, a user must only be able to see a form for updating their account details by invoking the userController.edit method when they are logged in. The route definition for the corresponding URL path /user/edit could therefore look like this:

```
app.get('/user/edit', restrictToAuthenticated,
                      userController.edit);
```

This tells the Express framework that when a GET request with the path /user/edit in the request line is received, it should first run it through restrictToAuthenticated, then pass it to the edit action of userController, unless restrictToAuthenticated prevents this.

We define restrictToAuthenticated middleware in a module called authentication. This module is shown in Listing 10. Like other modules we have defined for this application, authentication exports a function which takes a model class as its argument, so that it can access the methods of our User model. This function then returns the restrictToAuthenticated function itself, whose definition begins on line 3 of Listing 10.

Route middleware methods take three arguments: the request and response (conventionally given the names req and res), and a callback, usually called next, which is passed by the framework. Calling next passes control to the next middleware method, if any, or the action for the current route. Hence, a middleware method usually does something with either its req or res arguments, or both, and then calls next. Our restrictToAuthenticated method will only call next if the request is coming from an authenticated user.

The method defined on lines 3–13 of Listing 10 implements a filter that uses values stored in the session to determine whether a user may access the resource. It simply has to check whether the session exists and contains a user id in the expected place, which it does in line 4. If the test succeeds, all is well, the user is already logged in, and the next callback is called, which will normally just invoke the action that was requested. On line 5, before

Listing 10

```
 1  module.exports = function(User) {
 2    return {
 3      restrictToAuthenticated: function(req, res, next) {
 4        if (req.session && req.session.userId) {
 5          req.userId = req.session.userId;
 6          next();
 7        }
 8        else {
 9          if (req.method == 'GET')
10            req.session.requestedUrl = req.url;
11          res.redirect('/login');
12        }
13      }
14    }
15  };
```

calling next, we copy the user id from the session to a dedicated property req.userId, for convenience. If the test fails, the request was not sent by a logged-in user (or, to be more precise, it was not sent by a user agent which was storing a cookie holding the session id of a logged-in user's session). In that case, the requested URL is remembered, to be used when the user logs in, as we just described, and an HTTP redirect to the login page is sent. The effect from the user's point of view is that they will be asked to log in if they send a request for a restricted resource, unless they are already logged in.

There remains a small problem. After a successful login, the user will be redirected to the URL that was stored in req.session.requestedUrl, by sending a response to the user's browser with status code 302 (Found), which is the way that HTTP requires redirections to be made. (Arguably, status code 303, SeeOther, would be more appropriate, but not all browsers understand it.) On receiving this response, the browser sends a request to the URL it receives in the Location header of the 302 response. This new request always uses the GET method. As there is no way to redirect a POST request, there is no point remembering the URL for the restricted resource unless the request used the GET method, so on line 9 the request

Listing 11

```
 1  module.exports = function(User) {
 2   return {
 3    currentUser: function(req, res, next) {
 4     User.findById(req.userId, function(err, u) {
 5      if (err)
 6       res.render('error', {status: 500,
 7                 message: 'Server Error',
 8                 title: 'No Such User'});
 9      else {
10       req.currentUser = u;
11       next();
12      }
13     });
14    }
15  }
```

method is checked. The URL is only stored in the session if the method was GET. If you think about it, this is not unreasonable, because a user who is not logged should not have any way of making POST requests, as these will come from forms that are hidden behind the login. Any POST request that fails authentication is therefore probably suspect, so there's no harm in forgetting the URL in that case.

In the next chapter we will see that it is often adequate to have the id for the current user available to controller actions, but more often we need the User object that the id identifies. We can define another middleware function to retrieve the object. All we need to do is call User.findById, passing it the value just stored in req.userId. If the lookup fails, something is wrong – probably a corrupt session – so we give up and return a response with status 500 (Internal Server Error) and an error page to display. Otherwise, we store the retrieved User object in req.currentUser, where the controller methods for managing users expect to find it. The currentUser method is defined in its own module, shown in Listing 11.

Listing 12

```
1  var userLoader = require('./middleware/user_loader')(db),
2      loadCurrentUser = userLoader.currentUser;
3  var authentication =
4        require('./middleware/authentication')(User),
5      restrictToAuthenticated =
6            authentication.restrictToAuthenticated;
7  var restrictToAuthenticatedUser =
8      [restrictToAuthenticated, loadCurrentUser];
9  app.get ('/user', restrictToAuthenticatedUser,
10         userController.show);
11  app.get ('/user/new', userController.new);
12  app.post('/user', reject_duplicate_email,
13         userController.create);
14  app.get ('/user/edit', restrictToAuthenticatedUser,
15         userController.edit);
16  app.put ('/user', restrictToAuthenticatedUser,
17         userController.update);
18  app.del ('/user', restrictToAuthenticatedUser,
19         userController.destroy);
```

Express offers a neat way of combining route middleware methods. Instead of specifying a method in the route, we can specify an array containing any number of methods. This allows us to combine small functions to implement complex authorization logic, as we will show in the next chapter. For our user controller methods, we just need to use the two methods we have defined in this chapter. The way this is done is shown in Listing 12. The array of middleware that restricts requests to logged-in users and loads the User object is defined on lines 7 and 8, and applied to all the controller methods that must be restricted to the current user's data.

In order to enable any of this to happen, it is necessary to provide a login link on every page of the site. This should change to a logout link once the user has logged in. For this change to be possible, some means of determining whether or not a user is logged in is needed. This is trivial to implement: it is just the test which we have already used on line 4 of Listing 10. In an Express application, the test must be the body of a dynamic helper to make it available in any view that needs it. This is done as follows in the application's main program:

```
app.dynamicHelpers({ logged_in: function(req, res){
        return req.session && req.session.userId; }
    });
```

The logged_in method can then be used in the navbar template to determine whether to display a Log In or Log Out link.

If you want to support persistent logins, allowing users to remain logged in after they quit and restart their browsers, you only need to ensure that the cookie containing the session id has an expiry time, so that it is not deleted at the end of the current browsing session. The way you do this depends on the framework you are using. In Express, the session property of the request object has a cookie property, which allows you to modify the session cookie's attributes. In particular, assigning a value to req.session.cookie.expires allows you to set an explicit expiry time for the session. However, you should think carefully before doing this. It may be convenient for your site's users not to have to log in again every time they restart their browsers, but leaving them logged in puts them at risk if they ever use a shared machine. Never provide extended logins for critical sites, such as financial institutions. On the contrary, where security is paramount you should always force sessions to expire after a short period of inactivity, as we will describe later. Only allow users to stay logged in for extended periods of time or when their browser is not running if you can be certain that their convenience is more important than security.

In summary, to implement session-based authentication with passwords, several things are needed. First, a means of recording who may legitimately access the site and the passwords that identify them. This is the function of the User model and database table described in the *Accounts* chapter. On top of this model there needs to be at least a way for users to create accounts using a sign-up form, and a way of resetting passwords is more or less essential. Next, some means of storing session data securely between requests is needed. This will usually be provided by the application framework you are using, or by way of a plug-in. It is rarely necessary or advisable to implement your own scheme. A controller for creating logins, by displaying a login page with a form and then storing a user id in the session if the form is submitted with credentials that match a record in the database of users, can then be implemented as described in this chapter. Finally, a filter can be used before actions which access restricted resources, so that users are required to log in to perform those actions. The means of putting such filters in place depends on the framework being used. In Express, route middleware provides the appropriate mechanism.

Connecting the components of an MVC application, and arranging that HTTP requests are routed to the appropriate actions, is the fundamental purpose of Web application frameworks. If you want to see how all the pieces of our Express application fit together, you can download the complete code from Github, via a link at www.websecuritytopics.info.

Key Points

- HTTP is a stateless protocol.

- The need to remember whether a user is logged in is a specific case of the general problem affecting many Web applications – i.e. the need to remember state information between requests.

- State information may be passed between a Web server and browser in hidden input elements, modified links and query strings, or in cookies.

- When using cookies, the server sends a Set-Cookie header to the browser, which returns the cookie values in a Cookie header sent with every subsequent request to the same domain.

- The Set-Cookie header may include name=value pairs, specifying the name and value of one or more cookies.

- The Set-Cookie header may also include several attributes and their values, including expires, which sets an expiry data, and path and domain, which restrict the URLs to which the cookie is sent.

- The Cookie header returns the cookies in the same format, but omits the attributes.

- A session is an object or some other associative data structure, which appears to persist between requests from the same source.

- Cookies may be used to keep track of sessions.

- Elements of the session may simply be mapped to individual cookies, but limits on the size of cookies may be too restrictive, and the visibility of cookie data may be a security risk.

- A cryptographic hash can be used to prevent undetected tampering with cookie data.

- Sessions may be stored in a database indexed by a session key. Only the session key is sent in the cookie.

- The session key must be unique and unpredictable.

- Sessions are sometimes stored in temporary files, or cached in memory.

- Logging in is done by storing a user's id in their session. The session is checked for a valid user id when restricted resources are requested.

- Logging out is done by destroying the session.

- To prevent any possibility of eavesdropping, logins need to be performed over a secure channel, using HTTPS.

- If a restricted resource is requested and no user id exists in the session, the user must be redirected to a login page. The URL of the original request is stored in the session.

- After a user's credentials have been submitted, they are checked for validity against the database. If they are OK, the user is redirected to the page they originally requested, otherwise the login page is displayed again.

- To support persistent logins, ensure that the cookie containing the session id has an expiry time, so that it is not deleted at the end of the current browsing session.

- Never provide persistent or extended logins for critical sites such as financial institutions.

- Always force sessions to expire after a short period of inactivity for sites where security is crucial.

Attacks Against Sessions

Let us return to the analogy described at the beginning of this chapter. To gain entry to an office building, a visitor is asked to prove their identity and sign in. They are then provided with a swipe card which lets them come and go as they require without signing in each time, and which they retain until their visit is over. When they eventually sign out, they surrender the swipe card. If somebody wants to get in through the main door of the building without ever signing in, they have two options. They can make their own fake swipe card (if their forgery skills are adequate), or use someone else's genuine card. When access to a Web application is controlled by data in a session, the same options for breaking in exist: a hacker can manufacture a valid session, or they can hijack somebody else's session.

Before trying to manufacture a fake session id, it is necessary to determine what a valid one looks like. Typically, an attacker will create an account for themselves, using a fake or temporary email address, log in and inspect any cookies sent from the application, and look at any query strings that appear on URLs. Often, the fact that a cookie contains a session id will be indicated by its name, but it would be foolish to imagine that you can hide the session id's value by giving the cookie a more obscure name. When a cookie or query parameter is being used as a session id, it will be obvious to any but the most inexperienced attacker.

One way to try to manufacture a fake session is by brute force. Once the form of a session id (for example, a number or a hex-encoded string) is known, attempts can be made to access restricted resources using all possible session ids, generated systematically. These attempts will be made by a program, not a real person, so many requests can be sent in a short period of time. To defend against brute-force attacks, session ids, like passwords, should be long.

In fact, session ids should be very long. Nobody ever has a legitimate reason to type a session id, so the 4 kB limit on the length of cookies is the only restriction that affects their length.

Session ids should not be predictable, or an attacker could log in a few times under their own account, deduce the algorithm being used to generate ids, and predict a valid one that might have been issued recently to somebody else. In particular, you should not embed email addresses, IP addresses, the time of day or a linearly incremented sequence number in a session id. The entire id must appear to be random, not just some small portion of it. For instance, if you were to use the date and time and a random number between 1 and 100 as the session id, it would be feasible to use a brute-force attack, since only 100 values would be legitimate at any time.

These considerations suggest that a session id should be a cryptographic hash of a random quantity, used solely to look up the session data in the database. If sessions of that form are used, it will be hard, if not impossible, for an attacker to create a valid fake session. A session id is only valid during the time a user is logged in with that id, so the chances of a successful attack based on manufacturing session ids are slim. Hence, attackers are more likely to attempt the hijacking of an existing session.

Since sessions are digital entities, it is not necessary to take somebody's existing session away from them in order to achieve a hijack. It is sufficient to copy and use the session data, or just the session id. The challenge for the attacker therefore becomes that of gaining access to some other user's session data, while the problem for the application developer becomes that of preventing such access.

Some subtle methods of hijacking sessions rely on the abuse of JavaScript. These esoteric methods are described in the volume *Web Application Attacks and Defences* in this series. Here we will introduce some more obvious hijacking methods, to show how session-based authentication can be undermined.

If session ids are stored in cookies, copying a session id is equivalent to copying a cookie. Cookies are most exposed while they are being transmitted between server and browser. An eavesdropper who can intercept network traffic and analyse the packets will be able to pick out

Firesheep

Firesheep is a Firefox extension, released in October 2010, ostensibly to demonstrate the seriousness of the problem of session hijacking. If this extension is installed, all a Firefox user needs to do in order to hijack sessions is connect to an unprotected WiFi network in a location such as a coffee shop, and click a button labelled "Start Capturing". As soon as another user on the network visits one of the insecure sites known to Firesheep, that user's name is displayed. Clicking on the user's name takes their cookie and sends it in a request to the site, logging in the eavesdropper as that other user.

Although it was by no means the first program to do this, Firesheep attracted considerable attention and controversy, with many people seeing its release as an irresponsible act that allowed anyone to carry out session hijacking without difficulty – albeit only for insecure sites known to Firesheep. A certain level of technical sophistication had been required to use the previously available tools, but Firesheep made session hijacking simple when connections were not secure. At about the time of Firesheep's release, several prominent sites, including Hotmail, Twitter and Facebook, started offering their users the option of connecting to their sites using HTTPS exclusively. Whether this can be considered as Firesheep's having fulfilled its purpose is open to debate. At the time of writing, the Firesheep extension is still available and session hijacking remains a problem.

HTTP requests and responses, and extract cookies. Traffic analysis tools that can perform this task are readily available. The initial eavesdropping is not so straightforward to arrange, though. It can most easily be done on a wireless network. Some public access points, in locations like coffee shops or airports, are not set up securely – they may be entirely unsecured, allowing anybody to connect to them and sniff packets, or they may encrypt data using the obsolete WEP algorithm, which can easily be broken into. Many homes now have a wireless network, even if it only connects an ADSL router to one or two computers. Since the wireless signals have a range of at least 50m (and can be picked up from much further away by someone using a powerful antenna), it is entirely feasible for somebody sitting in a parked car with a laptop to intercept data on insecure networks in nearby homes. Intercepting traffic on a wired network requires a physical connection, so it is a less casual undertaking, but it can be performed by corrupt insiders or disgruntled employees. At a more advanced level, routers may be vulnerable to hacking. Once a router is compromised it may be used to intercept any data passing through it.

If a cookie is being transmitted, it's almost certain that the person sending it is logged in at that time. Thus, if the attacker can synthesize an HTTP request including a Cookie header with the intercepted value, they will be able to access restricted resources.

To show how an attacker might use intercepted cookies, we will suppose that Abelardo and Lady Gwendolen have signed up to Ninny's Tomb, a Freedonian Web service for star-crossed lovers with literary pretensions. Having found out about this, Gwendolen's wicked guardian Eduardo sees an opportunity to break up their romance.

Ninny's Tomb is hosted at the domain ninnystomb.com.fd. Eduardo's first task is to "map" the application there, that is, to discover the structure of URLs and opportunities for providing input, and generally to determine what the site does. He can do some of this using automatic tools, such as Web spiders, which follow all the links within ninnystomb.com.fd, creating a site map. To obtain more information he creates a Ninny's Tomb account of his own, using a false user name and a disposable email address, and logs in to the site. He is then able to discover how to send a confidential message to another member of the site. By inspecting the HTML, or by sending a message to somebody and looking at the request, Eduardo can find out how the data is formatted, the HTTP method, and so on. He is able to carry out all of this activity simply by using legitimate operations on the site, so there is nothing that the site administrator can do to prevent it.

With the knowledge gained from his investigations, Eduardo is now able to attempt to break up the sweethearts' romance by writing a small program. This program creates an HTTP request whose effect is to send a message to Abelardo, apparently coming from Lady Gwendolen, telling him that she can no longer tolerate his obsession with the game of tiddlywinks, and that she never wants to see him again. Sending this request without a cookie would cause it to be redirected to the login page, but sending it with a cookie that was being used to track one of Lady Gwendolen's sessions would make the message appear genuine, so that Abelardo would have no reason to be suspicious. In order to carry out this plan, Eduardo simply needs to eavesdrop on the wireless LAN in the family castle until he – or more precisely, his *packet sniffer* – finds a cookie being sent in a request to ninnystomb.com.fd. This eavesdropping software forwards the cookie to Eduardo's program, which then sends the damaging message. (This scheme would only work reliably if Lady Gwendolen were the only registered user of ninnystomb.com.fd in the castle. If members of the castle's domestic staff also used Ninny's Tomb, Eduardo could find that his program was sending a message purporting to come from the cook or the gardener, for example.)

In reality, attacks like this can be used maliciously to send spam messages to somebody's friends on a social network, or illegally to enable an attacker to obtain confidential information stored on a site, and possibly even to use somebody else's credit card to make purchases. (However, many e-commerce sites will only deliver to the cardholder's billing address, in which case this sort of theft can be prevented by administrative rather than technical means.) Crude attacks of this type can be prevented by only sending cookies over a TLS/SSL connection, using HTTPS. Since the entire transmission is encrypted in that case, the attacker cannot extract the cookie. There is, however, a significant overhead in using HTTPS, and it is common to restrict its use to critical areas of a site, such as the login page, a checkout, or administrative areas. This may mean that cookies might sometimes be sent in unencrypted form. Setting the Secure attribute of the cookie will prevent this happening, but to be entirely certain, the mixture of HTTP and HTTPS should be avoided by requiring HTTPS throughout the entire site.

Taking cookies from a public or shared computer is even easier than eavesdropping on a wireless network. Scrupulous Internet cafés clear down a system automatically once a user has finished with it, but smaller ad hoc operations and college facilities don't always take such precautions. Many users are not accustomed to clearing out cookies after using a browser, so it's quite possible to walk up to a shared machine and take over another user's session just by restarting the browser. HTTPS is no help here, because the cookies are not in transit. The only defence against unauthorized access of this type is for the application to expire the session.

There is no way to force a session cookie to expire. If a request is received from the browser, a Set-Cookie header that erases the current cookie can be sent in the response, but if the user has moved on and does not return, the cookie will remain in their browser. However, if the cookie's expiry time is set to a suitably short time after it is sent, the user will be required to log in again to gain access to restricted resources. This technique offers no defence against serious adversaries, though. Unlike a browser, an attacker who has intercepted a cookie can ignore the expiry time attribute, so they can use the value in a synthesized request for as long as they choose.

To prevent users being logged in indefinitely, the expiration of their sessions must be managed on the server. This is simple to do, by updating a timestamp on the session every time a request uses it. Before each update, it is necessary to check that the previous update to the timestamp did not occur longer ago than the permitted length of a session. It is up to the Web application's owner to specify how much time should be allowed in a session. Banking applications often force customers to log in again after a few minutes of idle time. Less security-conscious applications may allow them half an hour or more. No timeout greater than a few seconds can rule out the possibility of an abandoned session on a shared computer being picked up by an unauthorized user, but it can certainly reduce the opportunity substantially.

There are some subtleties to expiring sessions which require consideration. For instance, when a user whose connection has been idle for too long sends a request for a restricted resource, they will be redirected to the login page as if they had never been logged in at all. As before, therefore, the application must remember the URL of the request. In this case, though, it is quite possible that the request may legitimately be using the POST method. Suppose that ninnystomb.com.fd logs visitors out after half an hour of inactivity. Lady Gwendolen logs in to her account and starts to fill in a long survey, but the phone rings and she has to pause in order to talk to her mother for 48 minutes before she can submit the form. There is no way to redirect a POST request, so her form data is simply lost. If this has ever happened to you when filling in a long form, you will know how infuriating it can be.

Alternatively, imagine that Lady Gwendolen has finished what she was doing at ninnystomb.com.fd and is just about to log out when the phone rings. After her long conversation with her mother, she returns to her computer and hits the logout button. It would be equally infuriating, and very confusing for the user, if she is informed at this point that she has to log in again in order to log out. When sessions are timed out, it is necessary to make an exception of requests to the logout action.

Whenever sessions are stored in the database and accessed by a cookie, the session data can become orphaned – that is, the user quits their browser or the cookie expires, so there is no longer any way for the session data to be retrieved. To prevent old sessions clogging up the database, they should be garbage-collected regularly. The mechanism for doing this depends on the server-side technology, database, and operating system. On Unix-like systems, it is usual to run a cron job every night to delete records from the sessions table if they have not been accessed recently. This not only cleans up the database, but also provides a secondary mechanism for expiring idle sessions.

The possibility of cookies being intercepted underlines the inadvisability of storing any important data in a cookie. Unless the cookie is transmitted in encrypted form, data in it may be read by anybody who can intercept it. Even email addresses have value to spammers, who need valid addresses for sending junk mail to, and to use as return addresses in order to get past certain types of filter. Other information, such as passwords or even credit card details, is more valuable. When considering what data to store in a cookie you should take the most pessimistic view and treat a cookie as if it were readable by anyone.

If you decide that no harm can come from having your session data read, you should still make sure that it cannot be tampered with, by including a cryptographic hash of its contents which is checked when your application receives the cookie. Even if you do this, you may leave some types of application open to a less obvious form of attack, known as a ***replay attack***. In general, a replay attack may be the fraudulent or malicious repetition of any network transmission which legitimately authorizes a transaction just once, but is intercepted and repeated for illicit purposes.

Let us assume that one of the features of ninnystomb.com.fd is a facility for users to send digital gifts, such as virtual flowers and animated sonnets, to other members of the community. Because these virtual goods are very cheap, the only economically feasible way of organizing payments is for the site's users to buy batches of "gift credits" in quantities large enough to cover credit card charges. These gift credits are then used in small amounts to pay for the virtual gifts. Each user has an account, with a certain number of gift credits, and the number of credits is reduced in the obvious way whenever they buy a gift.

Suppose that Eduardo himself has a romantic susceptibility. While he is mapping the Ninny's Tomb site with a view to sabotaging Abelardo's romance with his niece, he discovers the profile of a literary lady who claims to be more lovely than a summer's day. Although smitten by love he cannot cease to be a miser and a cheat, so when he discovers that his account balance is held in a session, and a cookie is used directly to store the session data, he can't resist taking advantage. The cookie includes an SHA hash, so he is not able to edit it to give himself a million gift credits.

However, it is easy to do the next best thing. After buying the minimum permissible number of gift credits for ten Freedonian grotts, he makes a copy of the session cookie. (Some browsers have a built-in cookie editor, while others require an extension or an external application, but it is always possible to copy and change cookie values with very little effort.) Eduardo then sends the lady a virtual red, red rose, complete with animated poem by Rabbie Burns. After this transaction is complete, he returns to his cookie editor and overwrites the new cookie value with the one he saved earlier. His credit balance is thus restored to its original value, so it has cost him nothing to send the gift – and he could continue to send further gifts indefinitely, all for less than the price of a glass of Freedonian klurp.

The possibility of replay attacks should be sufficient reason not to include valuable data in a session that is going to be stored in cookies. If you feel that you have a compelling reason to do this, you must ensure that a cookie session can only be used once. This can be done by including a *nonce* (a unique value that is only ever used once) in the session, but it is not trivial to check that a nonce has not already been used, especially if the application is spread over a cluster of servers. The obvious way to perform the check is by saving each nonce in the database when it is issued, and marking it as used as soon as it is sent back. But if you are going to access the database to check sessions, you may as well store the session data in the database anyway. This also prevents potential embarrassments, such as Ninny's Tomb users deleting cookies and thereby losing all their gift credits, or logging on from a different machine and finding their balance has suddenly dropped to zero.

We said earlier that it is not necessary to take special steps to accommodate users who disable cookies, but other people take a less harsh view and do provide a fall-back mechanism, whereby the session id is passed in a query string appended to URLs. Links within the site are generated dynamically to include a query string identifying the current session. This method may be implemented easily in PHP, JSP or ASP.NET, for instance, but has the drawback from a security point of view that the data is visible as part of the URL. This is more serious than it may appear. For example, if a visitor comes to a page of your Web site using a URL which includes a query string with data in it, such as a session id – or worse, a user id – and the page has a link to some other site, the URL, complete with the session id or other data, will be sent in the Referer (sic) header to the other site.

Forums and blog comments provide a simple way to hijack sessions under these circumstances. Suppose that there is a blog at ninnystomb.com.fd, running on an Open Source blogging engine written in PHP. Eduardo could log in and leave a comment on some post, which included a link to a script running on a site he controlled.

```
<p>Great post, check out <a href="http://www.eduardos.com.
fd/">my site</a>!</p>
```

Comments like this are sometimes legitimate, or they may be a ruse to draw visitors to a phishing site, but often they are an attempt to hijack sessions. For example, suppose that Abelardo logs in to the site, with his browser set to refuse cookies. If it was running an old version of PHP (see below), the site might switch to passing his session id in query strings, which would automatically be appended to any internal links. In particular, a link to the blog page would be generated as something like this:

```
<a href="weblog/entries/latest?sessionid=2bb8da8a6ef21fd5f4e23
72">Lonely Hearts Club Blog</a>
```

If Abelardo clicks on the link embedded in Eduardo's blog post, the request that goes to Eduardo's site will include the following header:

```
Referer:http://www.ninnystomb.com.fd/weblog/entries/
latest?sessionid=2bb8da8a6ef21fd5f4e2372
```

Eduardo can easily arrange for the root URL of his site to be directed to a script which examines requests and extracts session ids from the Referer header. On finding a suitable header, Eduardo's script can then send a malicious request to ninnystomb.com.fd, incorporating Abelardo's session id in the query string. The request causes some undesirable action to be performed, as if by Abelardo himself. To allay suspicion, the script could return a 404 error, so that anyone clicking on the link in Eduardo's blog comment would just assume that it was broken.

As well as presenting such opportunities for session hijacking, URLs with query strings that contain session ids will appear in server access logs, which could be stolen relatively easily if a system administrator had failed to secure them properly. If someone, such as Lady Gwendolen, were to pass on such a URL to somebody else (easily done using the MailLink to This Page function provided by most browsers), the recipient would be logged in to the site as Lady Gwendolen when they clicked on the link which they received. Bookmarking a URL incorporating a session id is likely to have disruptive effects too. (As an added disincentive, think about how including session ids in URLs will affect search engine rankings.)

Being able to accommodate the minority of users who refuse cookies is not worth the security risks posed by using query strings to transmit state information in the form of a session id. Earlier versions of PHP (before PHP 5.3.0) used query strings by default when cookies were not available. To turn the feature off, it was necessary to set the configuration variable session.use_only_cookies explicitly to 1. This is the default for more recent versions of PHP. The CakePHP framework uses the session mechanism from the underlying PHP implementation by default, so if you are running CakePHP on an old version of PHP you will have to make sure that session.use_only_cookies is set to 1 in php.ini.

Express, Django, and Ruby on Rails do not support session ids in URLs. However, there is more than one Rails plug-in that adds this support, and plug-ins for other frameworks could be developed. Do not use any of these plug-ins.

Key Points

- When access to a Web application is controlled by data in a session, a hacker may attempt to break in by forging a valid session, or by hijacking a genuine user's session.

- Session ids should be as long as possible.

- Avoid embedding email addresses, IP addresses, the time of day or a linearly incremented sequence number in a session id.

- Long, unpredictable session ids that don't encode any guessable information are resistant to brute-force attacks and forgery.

- If a session id is a cryptographic hash of a random quantity, used solely to look up the session data in the database, it is very difficult for an attacker to create a valid fake session.

- If session ids are stored in cookies, copying a session id is equivalent to copying a cookie.

- Wireless networks – including domestic networks – which are not properly secured, may be vulnerable to eavesdropping.

- More advanced eavesdropping techniques are sometimes used against wired networks and routers, especially by insiders.

- An eavesdropper who obtains the value of a current session id from a cookie may masquerade as a logged-in user and access restricted resources in their name.

- Sending cookies over a secure connection using HTTPS prevents their being intercepted, but may cause an unacceptable overhead.

- Cookies can be stolen from shared devices if browsers are not cleaned up when users leave.

- To minimize the risk of cookies being stolen, sessions should be expired on the server. Care must be taken to ensure that this does not result in unacceptable loss of data from POST requests.

- When considering what data to store in a cookie you should take the most pessimistic view and treat a cookie as if it were readable by anyone.

- Storing certain types of data (e.g. credit balances) in cookies may allow replay attacks, even if a hash is used.

- Passing session ids in query strings is dangerous, since it allows sessions to be hijacked by way of the Referer header of any request from a link planted in the site.

HTTP Authentication

There is an alternative to issuing a cookie when a user logs in. Users can be required to authenticate themselves, by supplying their password each time that they send a request for a restricted resource. This isn't as onerous as it sounds, because it is possible to delegate the job of providing the password to the Web browser. To do this in a consistent way, authentication needs to be part of the protocol. HTTP incorporates two authentication schemes: ***HTTP Basic Authentication*** and ***HTTP Digest Authentication.***

Basic Authentication

HTTP Basic Authentication works in the following way. When a request is received for a page (or any other sort of resource) which is protected by Basic Authentication, the server looks for an `Authorization` header in the request. The first time such a resource is requested during a browsing session, there will be no such header. In that case, the server sends a response with status code 401 (unauthorized), which includes a `WWW-Authenticate` header. (The naming of these headers is unfortunately inconsistent and somewhat misleading, but is entrenched in the HTTP standard.) A typical example of such a `WWW-Authenticate` header is:

```
WWW-Authenticate: Basic realm="Authorized Personnel Only"
```

The value of this header begins with either `Basic` or `Digest`, indicating the authentication scheme being used by the server. It is followed by what the relevant standard refers to as a "challenge", which in the case of Basic Authentication consists of the keyword `realm` followed by an = sign and a string. This string is used as an identifier for a collection of resources, usually part of a single site, which are all protected in the same way. This protected subset of a site is called a ***realm***. In the example just shown, the realm is called "Authorized Personnel Only". The standard allows a response to include more than one challenge, but we will only consider the simplest case of a single challenge.

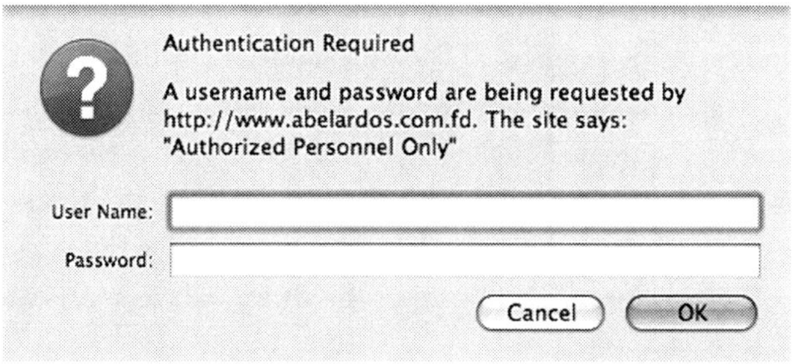

Figure 7. *Basic Authorization in Firefox*

When a browser receives a response with the status code 401 it displays a dialogue box requesting the a user name and password, which also incorporates the realm. Figure 7 shows the dialogue as it is displayed by Firefox. The wording and appearance of this dialogue are determined by the browser. Each browser's version is slightly different and the Web application has no control over any aspect of it apart from the realm. Firefox, for example, will always ask for a user name, even if users are identified by their email addresses.

After the user name and password have been filled in, the browser sends a second request for the same resource, this time incorporating an Authorization header, whose value contains the user name and password, separated by a colon and Base 64-encoded. A typical response to the challenge shown above would be:

```
Authorization: Basic YWJlbGFyZG86YmFzaWM=
```

The authentication scheme is repeated first, then come the encoded **credentials** – that is, the combination of user name and password. Although the credentials look nothing like a user name and password separated by a colon, it is important to remember that they are not encrypted, only Base 64-encoded to ensure they will not be corrupted in transit. Decoding Base 64 is trivial, so to all intents and purposes the credentials are transmitted as plaintext. We will return to the implications of this shortly.

When a request containing an `Authorization` header is received, the credentials it includes can be verified. If the user name is a valid one and the corresponding user's password matches the value sent in the request, the requested resource is returned in the usual way. Most user agents will then include an `Authorization` header with the same credentials in any subsequent request sent during the same browsing session for the same resource, or any other resources in the same directory sub-tree on the server.

If the credentials in an `Authorization` header are not valid, the server sends a 401 response with a `WWW-Authenticate` header, as it does when there is no `Authorization` header. Most (but not all) Web browsers remember that a previous `Authorization` header had been sent, and modify the wording of the dialogue which they then display, to indicate that an incorrect password or unknown user name has been supplied.

Basic Authentication is an example of a challenge/response mechanism. The `WWW-Authenticate` header plays the same role as the military sentry's question "Who goes there?", demanding a satisfactory response (which is supplied in the `Authorization` header) before an intruder may proceed. Figure 8 illustrates the flow of HTTP messages that comprise the challenge and response when a resource that is protected by Basic Authentication is retrieved. It is unfortunate that the challenge is sent in an HTTP response and the response in an HTTP request, but hopefully no confusion will arise.

The description just given glossed over how credentials are checked on the server. Because they are included in the request and response headers, it is possible for this check to be done either by the application or by the HTTP server itself. We will begin by showing how HTTP authentication can be integrated with user accounts set up as described in the previous chapter. This is done using code in the application.

We need to ensure that certain actions can only be executed if the request includes an `Authorization` header, with a user name that matches the

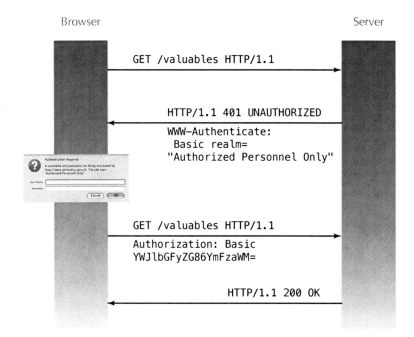

Figure 8. *Requests and Responses in HTTP Basic Authentication*

email address of a user in the database and the correct password for that user. We already know how to restrict actions to authenticated users: insert route middleware that performs the appropriate check. We can therefore implement HTTP Basic Authentication by rewriting the restrictToAuthenticated method we created for session authentication so that it checks the headers instead of the session. In this version, if authentication fails, we need to send the challenge in a WWW-Authenticate header, as we have just described. There is no need to implement any login action, nor to provide any page templates to gather users' credentials, because that is all handled by the browser.

Listing 13 shows the necessary code. Much of it is simply concerned with parsing the Authorization header to extract the necessary pieces so that the checkCredentials method of the User model can be called. As before,

Listing 13

```
1  require('../lib/extensions.js');
2
3  module.exports = function(User) {
4    return {
5      restrictToAuthenticated: function(req, res, next) {
6        var sendChallenge = function() {
7          res.header('WWW-Authenticate',
8           'Basic realm="Authorized Personnel Only"');
9          res.redirect('unauthorized', 401);
10       };
11
12       if (!req.header('Authorization'))
13         sendChallenge();
14       else {
15        var temp = req.header('Authorization').split(' ');
16        var authorizationType = temp[0],
17          encodedCredentials = temp[1];
18        if (authorizationType != 'Basic')
19          sendChallenge();
20        else {
21         var decodedCredentials =
22             encodedCredentials.base64Decode();
23         var temp2 = decodedCredentials.split(':');
24         var username = temp2[0], password = temp2[1];
25         User.checkCredentials(username, password,
26           function(err, u) {
27            if (!err) {
28              req.userId = u.id;
29              next();
30            }
31            else
32              sendChallenge();
33         });
34        }
35      }
36    }
37   }
38  };
```

we will pass the model to the function exported by the module, so that checkCredentials is available.

Like all other server-side frameworks, Express provides a means of reading and writing the header data in requests and responses. Both the request and response objects passed to an action have a method called header. For the request, this takes a string that should be a header name and returns the value of the corresponding header if it is present in the request. For the response, the method may take a second argument. If present, this second argument is used to set the value of the header. In particular, if req and res are the request and response arguments, respectively,

```
req.header('Authorization')
```

gives the value sent in any Authorization header, and

```
res.header('WWW-Authenticate',
     'Basic realm="Authorized Personnel Only"')
```

adds a WWW-Authenticate header to the response. The second argument sets its value so that the authentication method is Basic and the realm is Authorized Personnel Only. This makes it simple to add the required header to a response if authentication fails for whatever reason.

The little method sendChallenge, defined on lines 6–10, is called whenever it is necessary to send the challenge in the HTTP response. It creates the WWW-Authenticate header, and sends the appropriate status code in a response whose body is a page that simply contains a short message explaining that it was not possible to verify that the user was permitted to access the resource. Most browsers will display this document if a user hits the Cancel button in the dialogue that asks for their credentials. It will also be displayed by any browser that does not implement Basic Authentication.

When does sendChallenge need to be called? The Basic Authentication mechanism requires the challenge to be sent if the request for a restricted resource does not include an Authorization header, so the first thing we do is find out whether one is present, on line 12, and if it is not, send the challenge.

Otherwise, we need to check the credentials in the header. The call to String.split on line 15 breaks the header apart at the first space. If you look at the example header shown earlier, you will see that the first part should be the word Basic, and the second part the Base 64-encoded credentials. On lines 16–17 these are assigned to suitably-named local variables. The authorization type is checked, and if it does not have the expected value the challenge is sent.

If control arrives at line 21, we know that there is an Authorization header and its type is Basic, so we can sensibly decode the purported credentials, using our custom extension to the String object String.base64Decode, defined in the extensions.js module required on line 1, which you can download via www.websecuritytopics.info. We split the result on a colon to extract the user name and password (lines 23–24) and pass these to checkCredentials. (This code for examining the header is a bit long-winded in the interests of clarity.)

As always, checkCredentials takes a callback as its third argument, and this callback receives any failure or other error that may have occurred in its first argument. As in the case of session-based authentication, we store the user id in the request object, where it will be available to the action after next is called. Because of the way Basic Authentication works, this check will be performed on every request, so the user id will always be stored in this way. If the check fails, we need to send a challenge again.

Because the user id has been saved in the request object, as it was when we implemented session-based authentication, the currentUser method to retrieve the User object and store it in the request can be used without change from the version shown earlier in Listing 11.

This version of the `restrictToAuthenticated` method based on HTTP Basic Authentication is used in the same way as the previous one (which used sessions), by including it in the array `restrictToAuthenticatedUser` used in the route definitions for any action that accesses restricted resources. Within those actions, `currentUser` can also be used as it was previously. No additional modifications to actions are needed.

As we mentioned earlier, there is no need to implement a login procedure in the application. There is no need to implement logout either, because Basic Authentication does not provide any means of logging out. Once the browser starts sending `Authorization` headers, it will go on doing so until the browsing session is terminated.

Digest Authentication

When Basic Authentication is used, credentials are transmitted without encryption, so it is conceivable that somebody could intercept the transmission and discover user names and passwords. With the growth of public wireless access points and home wireless networks, which are not always properly set up for security, the risk of such interception cannot be dismissed. Passwords used for HTTP Authentication are particularly susceptible to interception because they are sent with every request. Where other authentication schemes are used, it is more often the case that the password is only sent when the user logs in, so an interceptor would only be able to steal a password if they happened upon the HTTP request sent at that point. (Unsecured cookies can be intercepted and used to hijack sessions, as we described earlier, but this is somewhat less of a risk than having passwords intercepted, because passwords are so often re-used on multiple sites.)

A guaranteed way of securing HTTP Basic Authentication is to encrypt all the data sent between the browser and server, at the transport level, using TLS/SSL. Sometimes this may not be practical, though, so **HTTP Digest Authentication** may be used instead.

HTTP Digest Authentication works in exactly the same way as Basic Authentication, as illustrated in Figure 8. The server issues a challenge, by way of the WWW-Authenticate header and the browser responds by sending credentials in the Authorization header. The difference lies in the contents of these two headers. Both challenge and response are more complicated than those used in Basic Authentication.

Here is a typical example of a Digest Authentication WWW-Authenticate header.

```
WWW-Authenticate: Digest realm="Securely Authorized Personnel
Only",
nonce="AAR+Ji6nI0M=68c20351c09a9cf2983dcf30a1cc2104c2f37adb",
algorithm=MD5, domain="/", qop="auth"
```

The first element of the header is, predictably, the word Digest, indicating the authentication scheme. As before, this is followed by a specification of the realm.

The next parameter is a nonce. The nonce sent in the WWW-Authenticate header is used to identify a specific challenge, so that, as we will describe shortly, the response to it can be identified. The contents of the nonce are not specified by the HTTP standard, but it must be uniquely generated. It is recommended that it be derived from a string that includes a timestamp, so that the server can not only test whether a response matches a challenge, but can also determine whether the challenge is sufficiently recent for it to be feasible that the response was generated by the browser on receipt of the 401 response, and has not been illicitly manufactured in some other way from an old HTTP message.

The algorithm parameter allows the server to specify a hashing algorithm to be applied to the credentials that will be returned. **MD5** is the default and the only option generally supported. The domain parameter is used to specify explicitly the URLs to which the authentication applies. In the example above, the entire site has been protected. Finally, the qop parameter indicates the "quality of protection" afforded by the server. This parameter is presently ignored by browsers.

The Authorize header sent by the browser is more complicated for Digest Authentication than for Basic, as this example illustrates.

```
Authorization:  Digest username="abelardo",
 realm="Securely Authorized Personnel Only",
 nonce="AAR+Ji6nI0M=68c20351c09a9cf2983dcf30a1cc2104c2f37adb",
 uri="/restricted.html", algorithm=MD5,
 response="3f820d9f2198fc1d9612a3de21db3753",
 qop=auth, nc=00000001, cnonce="01b6730aae57c007"
```

As with the WWW-Authenticate header, the first few elements are predictable. First comes the confirmation that the authentication scheme is Digest, then the user name is given explicitly, followed by the realm, as in the equivalent Basic header. After that, the nonce value is sent back, to confirm that this request is being sent as a response to the specific challenge issued by the server. The algorithm and qop parameters are also sent back. The URL is included redundantly in the uri parameter, so the server can verify that the request is for a resource lying within the protected area.

The response parameter is the important part of this header, as before. For Digest Authentication the value really is encrypted: it's an MD5 hash, but not just of the password. The full computation is relatively complicated.

First, the user name, the realm and the password are concatenated, with colons in between, and the MD5 hash of the resulting string is calculated. This value is referred to as *HA1*. Next, a second value, *HA2* is computed by concatenating the method and URL from the request, again separated by a colon, and calculating its MD5 hash. Finally, a string is constructed by concatenating *HA1*, the nonce, the values of the three remaining parameters nc, cnonce and qop, and *HA2*. Once again, these values are all separated by colons. The value of the response parameter is the MD5 hash of that final string. Fortunately, the browser does all the calculation.

What are nc and cnonce? They are additional values that are used to ensure that a request is not being "replayed", that is, copied and sent again by some program other than the browser that originally sent it. For further details of these values, consult RFC 2617, the specification of HTTP Authentication.

Now consider what you need to do to check Digest credentials in your own application code. The theory behind Digest Authentication is that the server has all the information that was used in creating the response, so it can compute its own value using the same algorithm and compare it with the value sent in the Authorization header. This means that the server needs to be able to retrieve the password, unless it has stored the MD5 hash HA1, described above. Storing plaintext passwords or using a reversible cipher to encrypt them is a serious security hazard, as we explained in the previous chapter, so using Digest Authentication commits you to storing the hash HA1, computed according to the specification.

Of course, there's nothing to stop you storing the password and user name in some other form as well, if that is more convenient for the rest of your application, but to deal with HTTP Digest Authentication you will need to store an MD5 hash that incorporates a user's password. Cryptographic experts now discourage the use of MD5, because significant progress has been made in breaking it. That may be sufficient reason not to use Digest Authentication. Using Basic Authentication over an encrypted connection is just as secure and presents fewer complications.

HTTP Authentication by the Server

The simplest way to integrate HTTP Basic or Digest Authentication with the creation and management of user accounts is by adding the necessary code to the application, as just described. However, as we remarked earlier, it is also possible to delegate the authentication to the HTTP server itself. Doing so is normally somewhat awkward, but it avoids the need to write some code, and under some circumstances it may provide an adequate solution. For instance, if a site, or part of a site, should only be accessed by a small number of select users, who cannot create their own accounts, setting up the server to perform authentication may well be the quickest and cleanest way of providing the necessary protection. If a similar restriction must be applied to a static Web site, server-based authentication is the only way to protect the site and require visitors to enter a password to access it.

We'll begin by considering Basic Authentication. Most Web servers adopt a scheme similar to that used by Apache. In its most basic form this uses a file to hold a list of users and their passwords, which are encrypted using a version of the Unix crypt program. The htpasswd utility can be used to create this file and add entries to it. For instance,

```
htpasswd -c /web/authorize/site_users abelardo
```

This command will create the file and add the first entry with abelardo as the user name. The program will then prompt for the password, and ask you to confirm it. Although the passwords are encrypted (only for storage in the file, it does not affect their transmission), it is still a sensible precaution to keep the file itself somewhere outside the Web document tree. Otherwise, it would be possible for users to download it and subject it to an offline attack.

Other users are added in a similar way, but omitting the -c flag, so that the existing file is edited. It would be possible, if a bit messy, to provide a Web-based interface to the password file, but usually it is edited from the command line as shown. This would be acceptable if there were only a few users.

The Web server must be instructed to use HTTP Basic Authentication. The precise way this is done depends on the Web server being used. For Apache, a series of directives must be added to one of the server configuration files. If the main configuration allows it, these directives can be placed in a .htaccess file in the directory that is to be protected. A simple example is the following:

```
AuthType Basic
AuthUserFile /web/authorize/site_users
AuthName "Authorized Personnel Only"
Require valid-user
```

Apache directives are not the easiest things to understand, but the meaning here is fairly clear. The first line sets the authorization type to Basic, that is, it turns on HTTP Basic Authentication. The `AuthUserFile` directive that follows instructs Apache to use the file just created to find user names and passwords. Next, the `AuthName` directive sets the realm string. Finally the `Require` directive stipulates that any valid user will be permitted, that is, any user in the file who provides the correct password. This directive can be used to restrict access further to specified individual user names. For example,

```
Require user abelardo
```

would only allow Abelardo access to the site. Other users would be rejected, even if they provided the correct password. It is also possible to create groups of users and restrict access to group members.

Using a file to hold user names and passwords becomes inefficient if there are many users. In general, this style of authentication is only used for small numbers of users so the performance is acceptable. (It is quite common, although not very secure, to have a single user name and password to protect a static site, and just to tell anyone who needs access what they are.) However, Apache is also capable of using a database for user names and passwords if better performance is required. For details of how this is done, consult the Apache documentation.

Performing Digest Authentication in Apache is just as simple as Basic Authentication, though of course the server is doing a more complicated job.

HTTP Authentication and AJAX

Many contemporary Web applications use JavaScript and the XMLHttpRequest object to update pages dynamically without the need to refresh the browser window, a technique usually referred to loosely as AJAX. (For more information, see *Web Design: A Complete Introduction*.) In effect, some JavaScript code is used to generate an HTTP request and to process the response.

These requests still go through the browser so, if the user has provided valid credentials, an appropriate Authorization header will be sent with each request. The authentication is transparent so HTTP Authentication does not usually interfere with AJAX.

It is conceivable that a site might use XMLHttpRequest to send a request to a part of the site that was protected from a page that wasn't protected. In that case, the user would not have provided their credentials to reach the page from which the XMLHttpRequest was sent, so the response to the request would have status code 401. If so, the usual dialogue will be displayed. It does not appear to be possible to intercept the response, display a custom dialogue from within the application, and persuade the browser to send Authorization headers with subsequent requests. This rules out the possibility of by-passing the standard dialogue and providing your own.

Seeing an authentication dialogue under the circumstances just described would probably be a bit disconcerting to the user. However, it would be an odd design that allowed it to be displayed in this way.

A user file can be created and edited using the htdigest command, which works in essentially the same way as htpasswd, with the minor difference that you must specify the realm when adding a new user. Digest Authentication is specified in a configuration file in a very similar way to Basic Authentication.

```
AuthType Digest
AuthUserFile /web/authorize/digestedusers
AuthName "Securely Authorized Personnel Only"
AuthDigestDomain /
Require valid-user
```

HTTP Authentication and Usability

HTTP Authentication is part of the protocol standard, is supported by most browsers, and is easy to implement, yet it is not the most popular way of adding authentication to Web applications. Part of this is due to the misapprehension that HTTP Basic Authentication is insecure because passwords are sent unencrypted. As we explained previously, it is no more or less secure than schemes which ask users for their password in a form. In either case, if the data is sent over an encrypted connection it is secure, but if the connection is not encrypted, the data can be read by anyone who intercepts the transmission.

Other objections to HTTP Authentication are based on considerations of its usability. Whenever a browser needs to obtain credentials for a site that requires HTTP Authentication, it displays the standard dialogue box that was illustrated in Figure 7, or its equivalent in another browser. The dialogue is not integrated into a Web page but is superimposed on top of it, and its appearance is browser-dependent and outside the Web designer's control, as is the wording of the dialogue. It may sound precious to complain about this, but having a dialogue pop up, which is in no way integrated with the site that is asking for the authentication, is inviting suspicion. In the context of authentication, this is the last thing you want. When a user is asked for a password, they must be confident that they are sending it to the site that they are logging in to, and not to some imposter. The standard dialogue, which is identical for every site except for the realm string, does not provide the necessary reassurance. Possibly, if everyone had always used HTTP Authentication, users would be accustomed to it and feel more confident, but this is not the situation.

Once a user's credentials have been obtained, the browser will send them with every request made to the protected area of that site for the duration of the current browsing session, that is, until the user quits the browser. There is no way for a user to log out, nor for the application to forcibly log them out, for example after a period of inactivity. For applications whose security is critical, this last omission is a serious shortcoming. Consider Abelardo using an online banking application from a shared facility, such as a computer in an Internet café or a workstation cluster in a college or office. If there is no way to log out, and Abelardo forgets to quit the browser when he leaves, the next person who comes along to use that machine can immediately gain access to Abelardo's bank account. It is essential that Abelardo be able to log out, and also that the bank's site be able to terminate his login if there is no activity for a period of time.

Conversely, HTTP Authentication provides no way for a login to persist beyond the end of a browsing session. Consider using a Web-based email service from your own machine. In this case, you want to be able to stay logged in indefinitely. You do not want to have to give your password every time you restart your browser. If you leave your computer running all the time this may not be a problem, but many people don't do that, and there is always the risk that the Web browser may crash. Other ways of implementing authentication make it possible to provide a "Remember Me" option, which allows users to remain logged in indefinitely.

Finally, because the authentication dialogue is not part of the application, there is no way to incorporate a link for resetting forgotten passwords. This function has to be provided on a separate page of the site itself. This means there must be a "Forgotten password?" link on the site's navbar, although it will seldom be needed. A link that only appears during login, which is the only time when it might be needed, is much more usable.

Because of these usability problems, there are many situations in which, despite its advantages, HTTP Authentication is not a suitable means of authenticating users, and more elaborate mechanisms are often preferred.

Key Points

- An application using HTTP Authentication sends a challenge and receives a response in the WWW-Authenticate and Authorization headers, respectively.

- When the server receives a request for a restricted resource, and the request does not have a valid Authorization header, it sends a response with status code 401, including a challenge in the WWW-Authenticate header.

- On receiving a 401 response, the browser prompts for a user name and password, which it sends in the Authorization header of a new request for the same resource.

- For Basic Authentication the challenge consists of the word Basic followed by the realm parameter.

- The Basic Authentication response consists of the word Basic, followed by the unencrypted Base64 encoding of the user name, a colon and the password.

- On receiving a request with an Authorization header, an application can check the credentials provided against the user account values stored in the database.

- For Digest Authentication a nonce, that is, a value which is only used once, is included in the challenge as well as in the realm and some other parameters.

- The response value is computed from the user credentials, the nonce, and additional values, and encrypted as an MD5 hash.

- The credentials can only be checked for validity if the application has access to all the values used to compute the response. This means that MD5 encryption must be used when user names and passwords are stored.

- Using either Basic or Digest Authentication, the credentials may be checked by the server. This allows static sites to be protected by a password.

- HTTP Authentication provides no means of logging users out or extending their login beyond a single browser session, and it offers no way of customizing the dialogue used for entering user names and passwords.

- HTTP Authentication is therefore not suitable when security is critical, e.g. in banking applications.

OpenId

The growth of popular Web applications requiring authentication means that more and more people are having to choose and remember more and more passwords. As many commentators have noted, strong passwords are hard to remember, so many people use the same password on several sites, despite the risks of doing so. In recent years, several attempts have been made to formalize the use of a single password for all sites, while providing adequate security. None of these attempts at creating a *single sign-in* service has gained universal acceptance, but at the time or writing, *OpenId*, thanks largely to its transparent adoption by some well-known Web services, is beginning to attract users. We will describe the operation of OpenId in some detail, mainly to demonstrate the difficulties associated with the superficially attractive idea of single sign-in.

OpenId is most easily described from the user's point of view, so let's suppose that Lady Gwendolen wants to use OpenId. Her first step is to obtain an identifier from an *OpenId provider*. Actually, for many people this step won't be necessary, because several popular services operate as OpenId providers, including Google, Yahoo! and Flickr, MySpace, Livejournal, Wordpress, Blogger and AOL. Many people already have an OpenId, therefore, though they may not know it. If you don't have an account with any service that operates as an OpenId provider, or you don't trust a company like Google to handle all your logins, you can sign up with a service, such as MyOpenId, which specializes in managing OpenIds. Lady Gwendolen preferred to do this, and so she obtained a unique OpenId from a Freedonian provider, in the form of the URL http://ladygwendolen.freedopenid.fd/. OpenIds usually have the form of an http or https URL. During the signing up process, she was required to provide and confirm a password. A password strength indicator was displayed to help her choose a hard password that was resistant to cracking. There was a CAPTCHA too, to make sure that she wasn't a robot. FreedOpenId offers a facility for recovering a lost password, as described in the previous chapter. This is important, because losing your OpenId

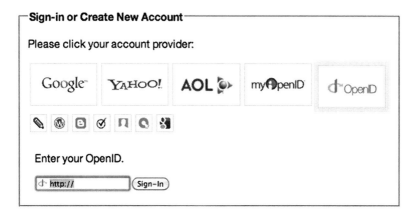

Figure 9. *An OpenId Selector*

password could potentially lead to your being denied access to many Web sites.

The Ninny's Tomb site supports OpenId authentication. Like many other sites, it provides an OpenId selector, in the form of a JavaScript widget like the one shown in Figure 9. This presents a list of well-known OpenId providers' logos, and allows the user to choose one of them and then enter their usual user name for that service. The OpenId URL is synthesized for them. Presenting choices in this way hides OpenId, and lets users believe they are just able to sign in using their GMail address, Yahoo! id, and so on. Users like Gwendolen who know that they are using OpenId can select the OpenId logo (at the right of the top row of icons in the selector). When Lady Gwendolen does this, the text field shown at the bottom of Figure 9 appears.

When Lady Gwendolen has typed her OpenId and clicked the Submit button, her browser is redirected to FreedOpenId's login page, where she logs in using the password she provided when signing up for her OpenId. The login dialogue tells her that she needs to authenticate for http://ninnystomb.com.fd, which is indeed the site she is logging in to, so she enters her password. Next, she is shown a summary of the information being passed back from FreedOpenId to Ninny's Tomb, as

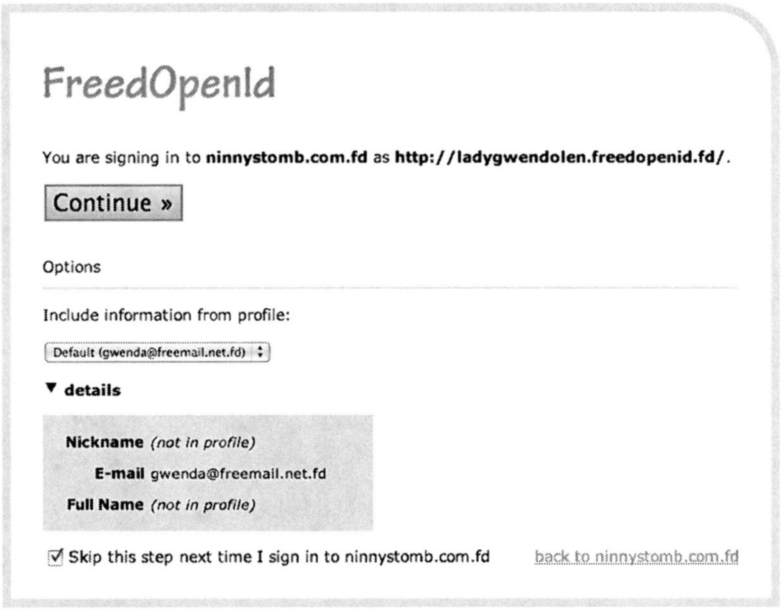

FreedOpenId

You are signing in to **ninnystomb.com.fd** as **http://ladygwendolen.freedopenid.fd/**.

Continue »

Options

Include information from profile:

Default (gwenda@freemail.net.fd) ⬍

▼ **details**

Nickname *(not in profile)*

E-mail gwenda@freemail.net.fd

Full Name *(not in profile)*

☑ Skip this step next time I sign in to ninnystomb.com.fd   back to ninnystomb.com.fd

Figure 10. *Logging in using OpenId*

shown in Figure 10. In this case the only information requested is her email address, which is taken from the profile she created at FreedOpenId. Having agreed to allow that information to be passed on to Ninny's Tomb, she is then redirected back to http://ninnystomb.com.fd.

As a user experience, this may not seem any better than logging in to the original site directly. If anything, it is slightly more trouble and could be confusing to a less experienced Web user than our heroine. However, there are several advantages to the single sign-in approach. To begin with, there is only one password, stored in only one place, so Lady Gwendolen gets the non-trivial relief of not having to make up and remember new passwords, without running the risk of one careless Web developer revealing her password and thereby compromising her accounts on many sites. It is reasonable to expect OpenId providers to know about security and to take adequate steps to preserve information and ensure that passwords are hard to guess, while other sites, whose main concern is not security, may be more lax. Finally, if it should happen that she discovers her password has been stolen, she only needs to change it in one place.

OpenId has some significant advantages for the Web site developer, too. It means that somebody else takes over the responsibilities of storing users' passwords securely, implementing a safe password resetting scheme, and preventing the creation of fake accounts by spammers. An OpenId provider should also be better equipped to implement additional security measures, such as two-factor authentication using security questions or smart cards, which would normally be too much trouble for an individual site operator to implement.

How does OpenId authentication work? Although we will continue to follow the customary usage and refer to the URL that you type when authenticating as "your OpenId", OpenId is really a protocol, defining the messages that must be exchanged to perform the authentication. At the time of writing, the current version is OpenId 2.0. As protocol specifications go, OpenId 2.0 is relatively simple, but it still has a lot of details that make it hard to implement from scratch. It is only sensible to use established libraries. These are available for JavaScript, PHP, Python, Ruby, ASP. NET, Java and other programming languages. An Apache module called mod_auth_openid is available, which allows OpenId authentication to be performed in the server, without adding code to the application.

To show you how OpenId authentication works, we will use the openid Node.js module to add OpenId authentication to the login controller shown earlier in this chapter. (If you were really adding OpenId to a Node.js application, you might prefer to use the everyauth module, which supports a wide range of authentication methods. Our example uses the single-purpose openid module as that makes it easier to see what is going on.)

Before adding the authentication, we shall extend the User model, to allow an OpenId value to be stored for each user and used to identify them as an alternative to their email address. This is not strictly necessary, since

OpenId does provide a way of requesting an email address from the OpenId provider when authentication is successful, as Figure 10 implies. However, we will adopt the simpler approach for this example, and assume that a column called open_id has been added to the users table. A property called openId, a corresponding private property for the persistentProperties array, and a static method called findByOpenId must be added to the User model to provide an interface to this value. We will not show the details, as the change is trivial and resembles the corresponding property and method for email addresses, which we used in the *Accounts* chapter.

Instead of adding the extra complexity of an OpenId selector, we'll just provide a single login page, offering OpenId as one option and the more conventional password as another. An additional text field is added to the login page shown earlier, with its name attribute set to user[open_id]. When the login form is submitted, the create action can check whether a value has been supplied in this field. If not, it proceeds as before to check the user's email address and password, but if a value has been entered, it performs OpenId authentication. Hence, we modify the create method exported from the login controller module originally defined in Listing 9, as follows.

```
create: function(req, res) {
 if (req.body.user.open_id)
  authenticateWithOpenId(req, res);
 else {
   // [ proceed as before ]
 }
},
 [...]
```

The method authenticateWithOpenId invoked here when a user supplies an OpenId must also be defined in the controller module, although it is not exported. Lines 7–19 of Listing 14 show how authenticateWithOpenId is implemented.

Listing 14

```
1  var openId = require('openid');
2  var openIdRelyingParty = new openId.RelyingParty(
3   'http://www.abelardos.com.fd/openid',
4   null, false, false, []
5  );
6
7  module.exports = function(User) {
8   var authenticateWithOpenId = function(req, res) {
9    var oid = req.body.user.open_id;
10   openIdRelyingParty.authenticate(oid, false,
11      function(err, authURL) {
12     if (err || !authURL) {
13      req.flash('error', 'OpenId authentication failed');
14      res.render('logins/new', {title: 'Login', u: null});
15     }
16     else
17      res.redirect(authURL);
18    });
19   };
20  // [...]
21  }
```

The OpenId 2.0 specification calls an application that allows OpenId authentication a **relying party**. The openid module exports a constructor for RelyingParty objects. When this constructor is called, it must be passed a URL to which the user's browser will be redirected after the first phase of the authentication is completed. We will need to add a route (/openid) and a corresponding action (validateOpenId) in the controller for this purpose. Since the URL is always the same, a single RelyingParty object can be created when the controller is first invoked. This is the purpose of the code on lines 2–5. The additional arguments to the constructor are all set to default empty values. They are only used for more complicated cases that we will not consider here.

When authenticateWithOpenId is called, it first extracts the user's OpenId from the request object (line 9). This OpenId is passed to the RelyingParty object's authenticate method, which also takes a callback, in the form of the anonymous function defined on lines 11–18. The second argument is a flag that determines whether OpenId's "immediate mode" is to be used. In immediate mode the user does not interact with the OpenId provider. If they have already been authenticated by the OpenId provider, the OpenId authentication can take place transparently, so the user does not have to leave the relying party's site. We will not consider that possibility, as it is less often used, so we pass false as this argument.

When the callback is invoked, it receives an Error object as its first argument, following convention. The second argument, which we have called authURL, is a URL supplied by the OpenId provider for performing authentication. This URL is called the *OpenId Provider Endpoint URL* or OP endpoint. The browser should be redirected to this URL, just as Lady Gwendolen's browser was redirected to FreedOpenId when she submitted the login form at ninnystomb.com.fd. It's possible, though, that no OP endpoint can be found. In that case, the argument will be null, so the test on line 12 fails only if everything went well – no error occurred and an OP endpoint URL was obtained. In that case, a redirect to that URL is sent to the user's browser.

The call of openId.RelyingParty.authenticate conceals a fairly complex interaction.

The relying party must discover the URL of the OP endpoint. This is usually done by treating the value that has been entered in the user[open_id] field as a URL and sending an HTTP request to it. OpenId 2.0 specifies the use of a "discovery protocol" called *Yadis*, which normally just sends such a request, but can handle more complicated cases, including those rare OpenIds which are not URLs. The body of the response may be an **XRDS** document (XRDS is an XML-based language devised for this purpose) containing an element whose content is a URL, or an HTML document with a link element in its head, in which case the href attribute's value will be the desired URL. This discovery step is necessary, because it may not be possible to determine the OP endpoint by examining the OpenId URL.

The next step is for the relying party to establish a secure connection to the OP endpoint. This results in the relying party's obtaining a secret value from the OpenId provider, which it can use to check that any further communications that purport to come from the same origin really do so. This step is optional, but should be performed unless the communication between the two sites is done over HTTPS, which means that it will be secure anyway.

At this point, after the callback passed to authenticate has been called, everything is set up for the authentication to proceed. The effect of redirecting to the authURL value passed to the callback is for the relying party to send a response to the user's browser with a redirect status code and a Location header whose value is the OP endpoint URL with a query string appended. This query string contains several parameters, most notably the user's purported OpenId and the return URL. These parameters are thus sent in a request to the OP endpoint, where the actual authentication takes place, with the user providing credentials to the OpenId provider, as we described.

After the OpenId provider has checked the user's credentials, it sends a request to the return URL, which was saved in the RelyingParty object when it was created. (In the example shown in Listing 14, the URL is http://www.abelardos.com.fd/openid). When the request is received, it causes the validateOpenId method, defined in Listing 15, to be executed. This method is included in the object exported by the module, so the Express router can be instructed to map the URL to that action:

```
app.get ('/openid', loginController.validateOpenId);
```

When the OpenId provider's request is received and the action is invoked, the status code is extracted to determine whether the authentication was successful. The action also needs to check the integrity of the response. Again, quite a lot is going on behind the scenes, but the openid module conceals the details. It just requires the RelyingParty object's verifyAssertion method to be called to do all the necessary verification.

Listing 15

```
 1  validateOpenId: function(req, res) {
 2    var badOpenId = function() {
 3      req.flash('error', 'OpenId authentication failed');
 4      res.render('logins/new', {title: 'Login'});
 5    };
 6    openIdRelyingParty.verifyAssertion(req,
 7      function(err, result) {
 8        if (err)
 9          badOpenId();
10        else {
11          User.findByOpenId(result.claimedIdentifier,
12            function(err, theUser) {
13              if (err)
14                badOpenId();
15              else
16                loginUser(req, res, theUser);
17          });
18        }
19    });
20  }
```

It takes the object containing the request just sent from the OP endpoint as its argument, so it has access to all the parameters sent back by the OpenId provider.

The verifyAssertion method takes a callback as its second argument, which receives an Error object and a result, as you might expect. The result is an object, the only interesting property of which is claimedIdentifier, which holds the user's OpenId. If there is no error, this value is used to find a User object (line 11). If one can be found, the user is logged in, otherwise the login page is displayed again, as it is if any error has occurred.

Once the OpenId authentication procedure has been completed and the user's credentials are verified, authentication of subsequent requests can be performed using the session, as in our earlier example. The loginUser function from Listing 9 causes the id of the User object just retrieved to be stored in the session, after which everything can proceed as before, with the restrictToAuthenticated and currentUser middleware from Listings 10 and 11 being used without modification.

The OpenId specification does not dictate how OpenId providers should perform the authentication. It is most common at present for them to use a simple password form, but they could also use certificates or any other effective mechanism.

If nothing else, the preceding description – which is by no means the whole story – should have shown you something of the complexity of OpenId and how it results from the requirements of a single sign-in service. Adding OpenId authentication to a real Web application would require some further work, particularly in the area of registration, but the basic structure shown above is enough to demonstrate some of the security implications. The protocol includes features that ensure the interactions between the relying party and the OpenId provider cannot easily be interfered with, and it uses a nonce to prevent replay attacks if the redirect is intercepted, but there is one major security weakness which is not addressed. To understand this better, let us return to Lady Gwendolen and her troublesome guardian Eduardo.

Eduardo would naturally like to know Lady Gwendolen's OpenId password. He finds an unscrupulous Web developer and pays him to create two sites: one that hosts a forum on romantic poetry and another that looks exactly like FreedOpenId's site. Anybody wishing to contribute to the romantic poetry forum must sign in, but they can do so using their OpenId. Lady Gwendolen, whose enthusiasm for romantic poetry knows no bounds, signs in to this new poetry forum. However, instead of discovering the OP endpoint for her OpenId, the site simply redirects her browser to Eduardo's clone of FreedOpenId's site, where she is shown a wholly credible copy of the FreedOpenId authentication dialogue. If she does not realize that this is a fake, Eduardo will soon have her OpenId and the matching password, and be able to impersonate her at Ninny's Tomb, and at any other site at which she can log in using OpenId.

At present, there is no defence against such impersonations beyond the anti-phishing filters built into most modern browsers, combined with common sense and vigilance on the part of users. Lady Gwendolen is unusually observant, so she noticed that the URL in her browser's address bar was `freedopenidd.fd` and not `freedopenid.fd` and cancelled her login, but not everyone is so careful. An extension to the OpenId specification, the **Provider Authentication Policy Extension**, provides a mechanism by which relying parties can require an OpenId provider to use a specified method of authentication. One way this extension can be used is to require a provider to use some anti-phishing technique. It can also be used by sites such as banks to require the provider to use multi-factor authentication (for example, a password plus a memorable name) or physical authentication – using a smart card, for example.

Adding OpenId authentication to a Web site may expose the site itself to an attacker with a sophisticated understanding of the protocol. Recall that the simplest method of discovering an OP endpoint is by sending an HTTP request to the OpenId URL. By entering a bogus URL on a login page in place of an OpenId, an attacker may trick the relying party into connecting to an arbitrary server, and perhaps executing a program with undesirable results. Alternatively, a denial of service attack might be made by using a URL that points to a large file, so that the relying party's server is tied up downloading it. Careful implementation of the OpenId relying party's code can prevent these problems, though. The best way to avoid them is therefore to use established libraries and not to try and implement OpenId from scratch yourself.

Once a user has logged in using OpenId, their session is vulnerable to attacks in the ways we have described in this chapter and others that use JavaScript. OpenId makes no difference, it is only a means of authenticating the identity of the user.

A different source of unease about OpenId concerns privacy. An OpenId provider necessarily knows all the sites that each user logs in to, and when they do so. This information could be of interest to law enforcement and security agencies and to marketing organizations, stalkers and anyone else wanting to track users' activities on the Web. Before adding OpenId to an application, you should consider whether you want to encourage your users to entrust this information to third parties with which you have no connection.

You will have gathered from the preceding paragraphs that there are some serious security and privacy concerns about OpenId. Nevertheless, there are also security advantages to having a single provider responsible for authentication, as noted earlier, and users may find the convenience of not having to devise new passwords all the time worth the risks. As a developer, though, it is necessary for you to remember that many users will not understand the risks involved, and so they are not able to make fully informed decisions about the safety and privacy of OpenId for themselves.

Further development of OpenId may make it more secure, but for now it is probably best reserved for uses that are not critical, such as logging in to post comments on a blog or forum, where no private data is accessible.

We will describe an alternative means of providing single sign-in in the next chapter.

Key Points

- OpenId is a single sign-in service that allows a single password and user identity to be used to access may different Web applications.

- OpenIds are obtained from OpenId providers, and have the form of an http or https URL.

- When a user obtains an OpenId, they provide a password to be used in conjunction with it.

- When a user signs on to a site using their OpenId, they are redirected to their OpenId provider's site where they are authenticated by providing their OpenId password and then redirected back to the site they want to access.

- When the user has provided their OpenId, the relying party determines a URL called the OpenId Provider Endpoint, using the Yadis discovery protocol.

- A secure connection is established and the user's browser is redirected to the OP endpoint.

- The OpenId provider sends a request to the relying party indicating whether the authentication attempt was successful. Extra information is included to allow the relying party to check that the request is legitimate.

- OpenId authentication is vulnerable to phishing and other attacks, and raises privacy concerns.

- Users may not fully understand the risks involved in using OpenId.

Authorization

As we explained at the beginning of this book, the structure of Web applications means that HTTP requests are the only way in which users and programs can invoke operations that create, retrieve, update or destroy resources managed by an application. A properly implemented system of accounts and authentication makes it possible to associate an account with every incoming HTTP request made by a user who has signed in, as described in the preceding chapters. There will be other requests, either from people who are not signed in, or from other programs. We shall briefly consider the last possibility towards the end of this chapter, but we'll begin by looking at requests that are sent by Web browsers.

The restrictToAuthenticated method which we defined in the previous chapter attaches a user id to the request object, so each request from a logged-in user is associated with the entity corresponding to the User object identified by that id. In many cases, whether or not an operation will be permitted depends on the particular resource or resources on which it is to be performed, as well as on the user requesting it. For instance, a user should always be able to change their own password, but never be allowed to change any other user's password.

To determine whether the operation being requested is permitted, it is necessary to have an efficient means of recording any restrictions that apply to each combination of operation, user, and resource. The authorization operation itself can then be implemented using route middleware.

Account-Based Authorization

The simplest authorization scheme to implement is one that associates the right to perform operations with individual user accounts. This makes sense if it is possible to identify an owner for each resource. Often, it is sufficient to identify the person who created a resource as its owner. In a typical case, each user with an account can create, edit or destroy his or her own resources within a Web application – but not those of any other user – and every visitor to the site can see some or all of any user's resources. In such a case, if operations on a user's own resources can be identified, the necessary authorization restrictions can be enforced. The simplest example of resources whose authorization follows this pattern is provided by user accounts themselves.

Managing User Accounts

All the data concerning a user who has an account will be available to the application as a User object, which persists as a row in the users table, so most conventional applications need to ensure that changes to such an object can only be made by its owner, or by a specially privileged administrator. More precisely, the application needs to ensure that any User object can only be modified or destroyed in response to requests that are associated with that object by the authentication method. We have already arranged for the currentUser method to find the right User object, so all that is needed is to provide URLs that allow a user to perform the CRUD operations on this object. We will consider the administrator's requirements in a later section of this chapter.

The operations themselves are implemented by the controller shown in Listing 4 in the chapter about *User Accounts*. That listing is annotated to show the form of requests that will invoke each method. From this, you can infer the URLs that will be used. The URLs were designed to assist in imposing the necessary authorization restrictions. To appreciate this, we must look at how URLs are generally defined in modern Web applications.

We have repeatedly described Web applications as managing "resources". Readers who are familiar with recent ideas about Web development may be tempted to consider users to be resources, in the precise sense in which that word has come to be used in the context of Web applications loosely based on the **REST (*Representational State Transfer*)** architectural style. In this sense, a *resource* is something which responds to a specific set of operations, invoked by way of HTTP requests. A representation of the resource, which may take the form of an HTML document, is sent as the response. These operations are usually called index, show, new, create, edit, update and destroy. This style of interaction maps comfortably on to the MVC pattern used by most Web applications built with modern frameworks: the state of the resource is stored in a model, a controller has methods for each of the REST operations, which invoke standard database operations (create, retrieve, update and delete) on the model, and suitable views are provided to display the resource's representations and obtain parameters to those requests that need them.

Using REST gives rise to the systematic pattern of URLs illustrated in Table 1. Certain URLs are used for more than one operation, with the HTTP method (or verb, as it is often called) being used to distinguish between them. In particular, the URL http://www.abelardos.com.fd/users/3 could cause one of three different actions to be performed on the User object whose id value was 3, depending on the HTTP verb in the request.

PATCH

The use of the PUT verb for requests that update a resource is well established, but it has been pointed out recently that using it in this way does not always conform strictly to its semantics according to the HTTP/1.1 standard. A PUT request should always replace the entire resource, but Web applications often use them to change just part of the resource. A new verb, PATCH, which allows partial updates, has been proposed in IETF RFC 5789, and some Web application frameworks now implement it, although Express does not at the time of writing. Like PUT, PATCH has to be faked by Web browsers.

URL	request method	controller method	operation
/users	GET	index	display a list of all users
/users/new	GET	new	return an HTML form for creating a new user
/users	POST	create	create the new user
/users/3	GET	show	display account details for the user with id=3
/users/3/edit	GET	edit	return an HTML form for editing the details for the user with id=3
/users/3	PUT	update	update the details for the user with id=3
/users/3	DELETE	destroy	delete the account of the user with id=3

Table 1. *A resource*

(The PUT and DELETE verbs are defined in HTTP, but are not allowed as the value of the method attribute of a form element in HTML, not even in HTML5 according to the current draft specification. However, there are well-established tricks for faking them, which allow applications built with most frameworks to behave as if all the possible HTTP verbs could be used in requests.)

The REST actions provide all the operations users normally require for managing their accounts. Users need to be able to update their account information by changing their password or recording a new email address. The combination of edit and update allows this to be done. They should also be able to close their accounts by destroying the corresponding User object. As we described in the chapter on *User Accounts*, they need to be able to sign up, using the new and update operations. A naive developer might therefore decide to map URLs to actions as if users could be considered to be resources.

URL	request method	controller method	operation
/user/new	GET	new	return an HTML form for creating a new user
/user	POST	create	create the new user
/user	GET	show	display account details for the current user
/user/edit	GET	edit	return an HTML form for editing the current user's details
/user	PUT	update	update the current user's details
/user	DELETE	destroy	delete the current user's account

Table 2. *A singular resource*

You will notice, though, that in the preceding paragraph no mention was made of the index operation, which displays a list of all the resources of a particular type. A user has no reason to see such a list (unless they are the administrator). Any individual should only be concerned with a single User object – the one for their own account. This is a sign that, in REST terms, the user should be a ***singular resource***, corresponding to the account of the user who sent the request currently being processed. That is, URLs that cause requests to be handled by the controller for users should act on a single User object only, and URLs need never explicitly identify a User object. Table 2 shows the pattern of URLs for accessing a singular resource. By comparing this table with the comments attached to each method you can verify that the controller shown in Listing 4 in the chapter on *User Accounts* was organized to operate on User objects as a singular resource.

To appreciate why this is more than a nicety of architectural dogma, think about the URLs that would be available if users were treated as plural resources, so that URLs followed the pattern in Table 1. Suppose each user was identified by an integer id. The URL to invoke the edit operation on user 3 would be http://www.abelardos.com.fd/user/3/edit, but only the user whose id was 3 should be able to invoke this operation. What is to prevent any other user sending a request to this URL? If such URLs are allowed at all, nothing would prevent it, so it would be necessary to include code in the controller to verify that the current user's id was 3. This would leave the question of what to do if it wasn't. It would also lead to the possibility of the application developer's failing to include such a test, so it is more secure as well as cleaner not to include the id in the URL at all, and always apply operations to the current user. This is exactly how a singular resource works, giving URLs such as http://www.abelardos.com.fd/user/edit, with no possibility of inadvertently allowing the wrong user to edit a record. The URL http://www.abelardos.com.fd/users, which would invoke the index operation on a plural resource is not allowed; it and any URL that incorporated an id, such as http://www.abelardos.com.fd/user/3/edit, should cause the server to return a response with a status code of 404 (not found).

If the current user is treated as a singular resource when URLs are set up, authorization will be performed adequately by ensuring that restricted operations are only permitted to logged-in users. We did that in the previous chapter by using the restrictToAuthenticated method of the Authentication module as route middleware. When restrictToAuthenticated is combined with the currentUser method to form the middleware array restrictToAuthenticatedUser, applying the combination to a route ensures that the req.currentUser property always holds the User object that has been associated with the request by whichever authentication scheme is employed. Authorization thus follows automatically.

The complete set of routes for the user resource is as follows:

```
app.get ('/user', restrictToAuthenticatedUser, userController.
show);
app.get ('/user/new', userController.new);
```

```
app.post('/user', reject_duplicate_email,
         userController.create);
app.get ('/user/edit', restrictToAuthenticatedUser,
         userController.edit);
app.put ('/user', restrictToAuthenticatedUser,
         userController.update);
app.del ('/user', restrictToAuthenticatedUser,
         userController.destroy);
```

By applying the authentication middleware to routes that correspond to operations on the stored resource, we have already ensured that users can only update and destroy their own accounts. Identifying the restricted routes and applying the middleware is all that is necessary to implement authorization for these actions.

Managing Users' Resources

In most real applications, users will own resources beyond the data in their accounts. The scheme developed in the preceding section can be extended to provide the necessary protection for any resources that can only be updated by their owners.

To begin with a simple example, suppose that the application provides a simple notice board where members of Abelardo's Tiddlywinks Club can post announcements. Any member can post a notice, edit it later if necessary, and delete it when it is no longer current. All members can read any notice, but no member can update or delete anybody's notices except their own. Only club members can read notices.

We first need to express the ownership relationship between club members and notices. Each notice has one owner; each user may own one or more notices. Using a term from conventional database modelling, we say that there is a *one-to-many relationship* between members and notices. There is a well-known method for representing such relationships in a relational database management system. The table containing the data pertaining to

Listing 16

```
 1  CREATE TABLE "notices" (
 2   "id" INTEGER PRIMARY KEY AUTOINCREMENT NOT NULL,
 3   "heading" varchar(255),
 4   "body" text,
 5   "user_id" integer,
 6   "created_at" datetime NOT NULL,
 7   "updated_at" datetime NOT NULL
 8  );
 9  CREATE INDEX "index_notices_on_user_id"
10   ON "notices" ("user_id");
```

a notice, including its text, has a column that contains the id value in the row of the users table for the notice's owner. (We will continue to use a model called User, with data stored in a table called users, to represent the club's members.) Conventionally, this column is called user_id, and is referred to as a *foreign key*. SQL select queries can be used to find all the notices owned by any member. Join queries can be used to find the account data for the owner of any notice.

Listing 16 is a suitable schema defining a table to hold information about notices. Each notice has a heading as well as its body (the actual text of the notice). We have added our standard id field and timestamps, and the important foreign key user_id. To speed up join and select operations we have also created an index on the user_id field.

We will not show the complete model for Notice objects. It resembles the User model from earlier chapters, but is simpler because it does not need to perform any encryption or validation. The values from the database are stored in private data properties, _heading, _body, and so on, which are initialized in the constructor from a hash of arguments and included in the persistentProperties array for saving to the database by way of the persistent_objects module. The argument hash includes the id value of the User object for the resource's owner, which is assigned to this._userId in the constructor. The value is saved in the database, recording the association between the notice and its owner.

Listing 17

```
var Notice = function(options) // Constructor

// Read-Only Properties
'id'       // The notice's id value
'updatedAt' // Modification time stamp
'createdAt' // Creation time stamp
'userId'   // The foreign key

// Accessor Properties
'heading'
'body'

// Instance methods
// Look up the User object for the owner and pass it to the callback
Notice.prototype.owner = function(callback)
// Look up the owner's name and pass it to the callback
Notice.prototype.poster = function(callback)
// Save the object to the database
Notice.prototype.save = function(callback)
// Return true iff the object has not been saved
Notice.prototype.isNew = function()

// Static methods
// Remove the object's data from the database
Notice.destroy = function(i, callback)
// Count the number of notices in the database
Notice.count = function(callback)
```

Properties are defined for accessing the values stored in the object. Most of these only have getters. The exceptions are the heading and body properties, which also have setters so these fields can be updated. The timestamps and owner cannot therefore be updated from outside the model. Whenever the object is saved, the updated_at field records the time and date. Listing 17 summarizes the interface to the Notice model. The standard methods are implemented using the methods exported from the persistent_objects module, as we described in the section on databases in the *Introduction*.

Visit the companion site at www.websecuritytopics.info if you want to download the code for the whole model.

We have not provided any methods in the model for retrieving Notice objects from the database. (That is, for constructing Notice objects using records retrieved from the database.) That's because we are going to retrieve Notice objects only when we are processing a request which is authorized to do so. Hence, we will perform the retrieval in a middleware method inserted in appropriate routes, as we will demonstrate shortly.

To begin with, note that all of the operations on Notice objects require authentication. The notices are intended exclusively for members of the club, so users must be forced to log in before they can even read the list of notices. That means that before we can consider authorization, we must ensure that the restrictToAuthenticated middleware that we defined in the last chapter is called for any URL that is concerned with notices. We won't be using the current user's profile data, so we don't need to call loadCurrentUser. In other words, we don't want to use the restrictToAuthenticatedUser middleware array to retrieve a User object, but only the restrictToAuthenticated method, which leaves the current user's id in req.userId.

We will do this using a neat feature of Express's routing system. Routes may use some regular expression operators, and a particular URL may therefore match more than one route. In that case, the routes are tried in the order they are written. If a route matches, the second argument to the routing method is called. This may be a middleware function. If so, when it calls next, as described in the previous chapter, control will be passed to the next route that matches. This allows us to group URLs together and apply middleware to every URL in the group. It would be simple to write an expression that matched any URL with notices in it, but we can do better than that.

By prefixing the RESTful URLs such as /notices/new with /user, giving URLs like /user/notices/new, we can indicate that notices resources always belong to users. We can then use the same convention for any other resource we might implement which has the property that each resource belongs to some user. If we do so, we can ensure with the following route that such resources can only be accessed through requests sent by a logged-in user:

```
app.all('/user/:resource/:id?/:op?', restrictToAuthenticated);
```

This stipulates that the `restrictToAuthenticated` method should be applied to any request, irrespective of the HTTP verb, where the URL begins /user, and then has the form of a resource name, optionally followed by an id value, optionally followed by the name of an operation. (The substrings beginning with a colon are placeholders, whose actual names have no effect on the routing.)

We can follow this with the route

```
app.get('/user/notices/new', noticesController.new);
```

If a GET request for /user/notices/new was received, it would first match the general route for all URLs prefixed /user, so authentication would be carried out. If the user was authenticated, `restrictToAuthenticated` would call next, so the next matching route – the one just shown – would receive control, and the new method of `noticesController` would be called.

Now consider adding the similar route

```
app.get('/user/notices/:id/edit', noticesController.edit);
```

Again, it matches the route that requires authentication, but that is not enough. Suppose the notice with id 147 is a plaintive note from Lady Gwendolen asking whether anyone has found her lucky purple squidger, which she mislaid at last Friday's tiddlywinks tournament. If Gwendolen subsequently finds the missing squidger and wants to amend the notice to let people know, she would log in, select the notice from a list, and click an edit button. (Don't worry about the details of the interface.) This would cause her browser to send a GET request for the form for editing notices. The path in this request would be /user/notices/147/edit. Her request would be successfully authenticated and the form would be displayed, with its action attribute set to /user/notices/147 so that submitting it would cause her notice to be updated.

There is nothing to stop any other logged-in user sending a GET request to /user/notices/147/edit and submitting the form. Suppose Lady Gwendolen's wicked guardian Eduardo had joined the club under the pseudonym Montmorency Worthyngton-Smythe. He could log in and read Gwendolen's notice, probably by clicking on a link in the list of all notices. This would cause the notice to be displayed, and the URL http://www.abelardos.com.fd/user/notices/147 to be shown in his browser's address bar. He could then type /edit on the end of the URL and hit return, to be shown the form for editing Gwendolen's notice. He is logged in, so his request passes authentication and he would be able to change the form into a scathing critique of Abelardo's dismal attempt at the John Lennon Memorial Shot in the same tournament. (If Eduardo couldn't guess the form of URLs for editing notices, he could have created a notice of his own and edited it, noting the form of URL. Obscuring the form of URL by choosing a suffix like /octopus instead of /edit provides no security at all.)

What is wrong here is that we are performing authentication but not authorization. Fortunately, this is easily rectified .

We need to ensure that within the controller's methods only the resources that should be allowed to the current user are available. We'll do that by interposing a second layer of middleware between the authentication and the actual controller methods.

Our strategy will be to build up a query that implements the necessary restrictions in additional middleware interposed before a method that retrieves data. Building a complex restriction may take several steps. At each step, the partially-built query will be stored in the request object, so that later middleware methods can add to it. There is nothing special about this object, so there is nothing to prevent properties being added to it, even though they were not actually part of the original request. This may seem inelegant, but the practice is well established, and it can be rationalized by supposing that the data logically belongs to the request, even though it was not sent over the network.

Finally, the resource loader will pass the complete query it finds in the request object to an appropriate method from the persistent_objects module. This will retrieve the desired records, which will be available to the controller method in the request object, in the same way as the current user object was passed into the controller earlier.

We will implement the restriction by combining the route middleware just described with URLs designed to limit the scope of requests, as we did in the case of User objects. For example, we want to be able to define the routes for editing and deleting a notice to use a middleware array which ensures that only the notice's owner can perform the operation. If we assume that there is such an array, assigned to restrictToOwnersNotice, we could use the following routes.

```
app.get ('/user/notices/:id/edit', restrictToOwnersNotice,
noticesController.edit);
app.put ('/user/notices/:id', restrictToOwnersNotice,
noticesController.update);
app.del ('/user/notices/:id', restrictToOwnersNotice,
noticesController.destroy);
```

There is scope for building the middleware array in different ways. We chose to construct it from small pieces, each of which performs a single sub-task. For example, the version of restrictToOwnersNotice which we use is as follows:

```
[allNotices, oneNotice, usersNotice, loadOneNotice]
```

The first three methods build a query, while the last one executes it to retrieve some records. The intention is that allNotices will initialize a query with no restrictions, so that if it was used in isolation all the notices would be retrieved. The method oneNotice adds a clause restricting the retrieval to a single notice, specified by its id value, while usersNotice adds a further restriction so that the retrieval will only return a record if the user_id field in the database matches the current user's id.

To help us avoid repetition, we will write the relevant methods in such a way that they will work for any type of resource that is owned by a user, that is, that has a user_id foreign key. We have arranged that any request for a resource requiring authorization will have been processed by restrictToAuthenticated first, so when the authorization methods are called, the current user's id will be available in the request, as req.userId. Furthermore, because of the way the routes are defined using placeholders, we know that when a record with a specific id is referred to in a request, that id value will be available as req.param('id').

Express middleware doesn't leave us much choice about how to pass values from one method to the next. We can only do it easily by storing the values in properties of the request object. In the end we need two values: a where clause with ? placeholders, as used in a prepared statement, and an array of values to replace those placeholders. We will pass these between our methods in req.dbQuery and req.dbQueryValues, respectively.

Listing 18 shows a module, which we will call authorization_filters, defining a suitable collection of methods for constructing query fragments to restrict the records retrieved from a table. The actual code requires little comment. (We will explain why the module exports a function instead of the collection of methods in the next section.) We don't want to make unnecessary assumptions about the context in which each method will be called so, as we build the string, we have to check whether we are appending to an existing fragment, in which case we need to insert an and operator before the new fragment, on lines 11–12 and 19–20. We use the Array.push method to add the values to the end of the array in req.dbQueryValues

Listing 18

```
1  module.exports = function() {
2   return {
3    allResources: function(req, res, next) {
4      req.dbQuery = '';
5      req.dbQueryValues = [];
6      next();
7    },
8
9    whereId: function(req, res, next) {
10     var queryPart = ' id = ?';
11     req.dbQuery = req.dbQuery?
12                  req.dbQuery + ' and ' + queryPart: queryPart;
13     req.dbQueryValues.push(req.param('id'));
14     next();
15    },
16
17    whereUser: function(req, res, next) {
18     var queryPart = ' user_id = ?';
19     req.dbQuery = req.dbQuery?
20                  req.dbQuery + ' and ' + queryPart: queryPart;
21     req.dbQueryValues.push(req.userId);
22     next()
23    }
24   }
25  }
```

to ensure that they are in the right order to match the placeholders in the prepared query.

These methods allow us to define the first three middleware methods needed by restrictToOwnersNotice.

```
var noticeAuthorization =
        require('./middleware/authorization_filters')(),
  allNotices = noticeAuthorization.allResources,
  oneNotice = noticeAuthorization.whereId,
  usersNotice = noticeAuthorization.whereUser;
```

Listing 19

```
 1  module.exports = function(resource) {
 2
 3    var persistentResource = require('../lib/persistent_
objects')(resource);
 4    return {
 5      loadOne: function(req, res, next) {
 6        persistentResource.findOneObject(req.dbQuery,
 7          req.dbQueryValues,
 8          function(err, theResource) {
 9            if (err)
10              res.render('error', {status: 500,
11                        message: 'Server Error',
12                        title: 'Server Error',
13                        layout: 'blank-layout'});
14            else
15              if (!theResource)
16                res.render('notfound', {status: 404,
17                          message: 'Not Found',
18                          title: 'Page Not Found',
19                          layout: 'blank-layout'})
20              else {
21                req.resource = theResource;
22                req.myResource = theResource.userId == req.userId;
23                next();
24              }
25          });
26      },
27
```

This just leaves us with the job of executing the query to retrieve records.

There are two types of route to consider – those which reference a single resource and those which reference all the resources of a particular type – so we need to define two middleware methods loadOne and loadMany.

The definitions are fairly trivial, as these methods can be defined in terms of the findOneObject and findManyObjects methods exported by the

Listing 19 continued

```
28    loadMany: function(req, res, next) {
29     persistentResource.findManyObjects(req.dbQuery,
30       req.dbQueryValues,
31       function(err, theResources) {
32        if (err)
33          res.render('error', {status: 500,
34                       message: 'Server Error',
35                       title: 'Server Error',
36                       layout: 'blank-layout'});
37        else {
38          req.resources = theResources;
39          next();
40        }
41      });
42    }
43   };
44  }
```

persistent_objects module, as described in the *Introduction*. The module shown in Listing 19 exports a function which takes a constructor as its argument, so the methods are bound to an appropriate model in a way which will be familiar by now. On line 3, we create a persistent version of the resource so that we can use the generic finder methods.

The preceding middleware methods store a where clause, with placeholders as used in a prepared statement, in req.dbQuery. The middleware also stores an array of values to replace those placeholders in req.dbQueryValues. Hence, all that needs to be done is to pass these values to the relevant methods of the persistentResource object, as we do on lines 6 and 31.

There remain only two problems. How are the retrieved resources to be passed on to the controller? And what should be done if no resources can be retrieved under the restriction specified by the where clause?

The only available solution to the first of these problems is once again to attach the resources to the request object. Hence, on lines 21 and 38, each of which appears within a callback being passed to a retrieval method, we either assign a single resource object to req.resource or an array of them to req.resources. Our controller methods will use these properties to access resources. They will never retrieve them directly, so only resources that have been "approved" by the authorization methods will be available inside the controller.

In the case of a single resource, it may be helpful for the controller to be able to determine whether the resource that has been retrieved belongs to the current user. This can be done by comparing the value of the resource's userId property with the current user's id, which is available in the request, so on line 22 we assign the result of comparing these two to a Boolean value which we also store in the request.

What if a database query fails to retrieve any resources? In the case where we are retrieving a set of resources, we can just assign an empty array to req.resources and leave the controller to cope with it. However, if we are only trying to retrieve a single resource, the situation is different. If no restriction is being imposed (that is, no authorization filters preceded the call of loadOne), the failure to retrieve a resource means that the URL in the request included an id that did not match any resource in the database. In other words, the resource being requested could not be found, so a 404 error should be returned. We do this by rendering a special page, setting the status to 404 (lines 16–19). If the retrieval is restricted, though, it is possible (in fact, it is likely) that the resource is there, but it does not belong to the current user. As our code stands, the result will be the same: a 404 error. In a way, this makes sense, providing you are prepared to interpret the request as searching for a resource with a given id belonging to the current user. If no such resource exists, it cannot be found, just as a page that does not exists cannot be found.

You may take issue with this approach and argue that the status code should reflect the state of the resource, so we ought to distinguish between resources that are not in the database at all and those that do not belong to the current user. In that case, the appropriate status code would be 403

(Forbidden) and a different page should be rendered, politely informing the user that they have requested a resource which they do not have permission to access. We don't consider distinguishing the two cases to be sufficient reason for performing a redundant database operation or retrieving data that would immediately be discarded. Furthermore, it is conceivable that being able to discover whether a resource existed or not might be valuable information to somebody trying to break in to the site.

We can use one of the methods from Listing 19 to provide the missing piece of middleware needed by restrictToOwnersNotice.

```
var noticeLoader =
    require('./middleware/resource_loader')(Notice);
var loadOneNotice = noticeLoader.loadOne,
    loadManyNotices = noticeLoader.loadMany;
```

(We will show an example of the use of loadManyNotices later.)

The combination of route middleware we have now defined is sufficient to restrict access to operations on notices, using the routes we showed previously. No authorization needs to be applied to the new and create actions, as these do not access any existing notice. If it is intended that any logged-in user can see all the notices, we do not need to apply authorization to the route for the show or index actions, either. It is sufficient to authenticate the current user for these operations. Remember that authentication will be applied before authorization by way of the generic route for all URLs that begin /user. In the next section, we will consider what needs to be done if each logged-in user can only see some of the notices.

With the authorization in place, a controller and some views for notices can safely be written, in the knowledge that the resource objects arriving in the request object belong to the current user, in the case of the edit, create and destroy methods. For instance, the edit method can be as simple as this:

```
edit: function(req, res) {
 res.render('notices/edit', {title: 'Edit Notice',
                                  n: req.resource})
}
```

The form will only ever be displayed to allow a user to edit one of his or her own notices.

Let us return to the example that motivated this treatment of authorization. Suppose Lady Gwendolen's user id is 12, and that she posted the notice with id 147. That means that the value of the user_id field in the record in the notices table with the id of 147 will be 12. When Gwendolen sends a request to the URL http://www.abelardos.com.fd/user/notices/147/edit, the path will first be matched against the route

```
app.all('/user/:resource/:id?/:op?', restrictToAuthenticatedUser)
```

Therefore, the authentication method restrictToAuthenticated will be called first. If she is logged in, as determined by examining the session, loadCurrentUser will be called immediately, otherwise she will be required to provide her credentials. Either way, the value of req.userId will be 12 when control is passed to the next matching route

```
app.get ('/user/notices/:id/edit', restrictToOwnersNotice,
noticesController.edit)
```

Remember that restrictToOwnersNotice comprises the array of methods [allNotices, oneNotice, usersNotice, loadOneNotice], each of which was imported from the authorization_filters module when it was passed the Notice model as an argument. Thus, the first thing that happens is that the allResources method is called to initialize req.dbQuery and req.dbQueryValues to an empty string and an empty array, respectively. Next, since oneNotice is a synonym for whereId, that method is called, leaving req.dbQuery equal to 'id = ?' and req.dbQueryValues equal to [147], picking up the id value from req.param('id'). The next filter performs the actual authorization. When whereUser is called, it augments the query so that req.dbQuery becomes 'id = ? and user_id = ?' and req.dbQueryValues contains the placeholders to [147, 12].

This means that when loadOneNotice is called and the values are interpolated into the query string, the effect is that of executing the SQL statement

select * from notices where id = 147 and user_id = 12;

Since the user_id field of the record with id equal to 147 is 12, the record is retrieved and displayed in the form for editing.

If, on the other hand, a request is sent to the same URL by Eduardo, whose user id is 13, the query will be

select * from notices where id = 147 and user_id = 13;

and no record will be retrieved, since none can satisfy both parts of the where clause.

The controller and views for notices are essentially trivial, so we will not show them here. The index action causes a list of notice titles to be shown to any logged-in user. Clicking on a title displays the full notice, the name of its poster, and the date it was posted. By using the myResource flag that is planted by loadOneNotice, we can display links for editing and deleting the notice if it is being viewed by its owner and not otherwise. You should realize that this selective display of the links does not provide any security at all. A user wanting to edit somebody else's notice does not need a link on the site in order to construct and send a suitable request. Never assume that requests have been sent by clicking a link. All requests must be authorized, and this is what the middleware arrangement we have described does. It will not be possible for Eduardo to edit Lady Gwendolen's notice by sending a PUT request to invoke the update action, for example, because we have made sure that the middleware array restrictToOwnersNotice is interposed before any vulnerable action.

Other Frameworks

The precise way in which we have implemented authentication and authorization as route middleware depends on the facilities provided by Express, the framework we have chosen to use for our example code. Other frameworks offer slightly different ways of achieving the same result. (We do not recommend implementing a Web application of any complexity without the help of some framework.)

Django supports middleware that can modify incoming requests. Django's middleware components are Python classes conforming to a standard interface. Each such class implements a set of methods that can modify the request or response at different phases in the processing. These methods return the modified object, which makes for a more elegant model than that provided by Express, but the strategy for providing authentication and authorization by inserting middleware to intercept incoming requests is identical to that which we have described for Express.

Ruby on Rails originally took a slightly different approach, using methods called filters. In each Rails controller (a class with methods for each action), it is possible to declare that a filter should be executed before a controller method is executed. Filters can be specified for all or just some of the methods. Functionally, this system is identical to our use of middleware, but the need to list the filters within the controller provides less separation between the authorization and the application logic. Recent versions of Rails make use of Rack, a standard interface between Web servers and Ruby frameworks. Rack supports middleware that is similar to Django middleware, consisting of classes with a standard interface that allows the request and response to be modified. Rack middleware is used for authentication and authorization in combination with several different Ruby frameworks, including Rails and Sinatra.

RailwayJS, a higher-level JavaScript framework built on top of Express, copies the idea of controller filters from Rails, which seems like a retrograde step.

PHP frameworks, with the exception of the Slim micro-framework which implements a system similar to that in Express, do not appear to have embraced the middleware concept. Other frameworks use filters, or simply rely on the programmer to call a function from the controller method itself to check whether a user is logged in or has permission to execute the action.

Controlling Access to Other Users' Resources

The general scheme we described in detail in the preceding section is highly flexible. It can easily be adapted to cope with different authorization requirements.

For example, it is common for the owner of a resource to specify that it can only be read or changed by certain other users. Suppose that, after the notice board has been in use for a while, the members of Abelardo's tiddlywinks club think that it would be nice to be able to use the site for exchanging private messages with each other, as well as for publishing notices for all members to see.

In this scenario, a user could add the addresses of one or more other members to a notice as recipients. Only those members would be able to read the notice, or see it in the list of their notices. Notices without any recipients would be public and readable by any member, just like the notices we have been working with until now. It would continue to be the case that a notice could only be edited or deleted by its owner, that is, the person who originally created it.

Based on the previous section, you should be able to see that we can ensure that members can only read the notices intended for them by adding some middleware to the routes for the index and show actions in the notices controller. Assuming we could use some as-yet-undefined export from the authorization_filters module to create a method called receivedNotice, which modified a query so that only public notices and those addressed to the current user were retrieved, we could define two arrays:

```
var restrictToReceivedNotices = [allNotices, receivedNotice,
                                 loadManyNotices],
    restrictToReceivedNotice = [allNotices, oneNotice,
                                receivedNotice, loadOneNotice];
```

These would then be used by the relevant routes:

```
app.get ('/user/notices',
         restrictToReceivedNotices, noticesController.index);
app.get ('/user/notices/:id',
         restrictToReceivedNotice, noticesController.show);
```

The implementation of receivedNotice depends on our having a way of recording which club members may legitimately read any particular notice. Any notice may have many recipients, and each member may be one of the recipients of many messages, so there is a **many-to-many relationship** between notices and members. Again, there is a well-established way of representing such relationships in a relational database.

We create a new table, which we will call notices_readers, having just two fields user_id and notice_id, holding foreign keys for a user and a notice. The user identified by the user_id value is one of the recipients of the notice which has an id equal to the notice_id value in notices_readers. In other words, the notices_readers table records which users are authorized to read each notice that has an explicit list of recipients.

We could retrieve all the notices that Lady Gwendolen, whose user id is 12, could legitimately read using the following SQL query:

```
select * from notices where
  (not exists
   (select * from notices_readers where notice_id = notices.id)
 or
  id in
   (select notice_id from notices_readers where user_id = 12))
```

Similarly, we could retrieve the notice with id 147 if and only if it could be read by Lady Gwendolen using the following SQL query:

```
select * from notices where
   id = 147
  and
  (not exists
   (select * from notices_readers where notice_id = notices.id)
 or
  id in
   (select notice_id from notices_readers where user_id = 12))
```

In both queries, the sub-clause

```
not exists
 (select * from notices_readers where notice_id = notices.id)
```

is satisfied by any notice that does not have an entry in notices_readers – that is, all the notices without named recipients, which can be read by any member of the club. The other sub-clause is satisfied by all the notices whose id appears in notices_readers associated with the user id we specify, in this case 12. The two sub-clauses are combined with the or operator, so the combined clause is only satisfied by the notices that Lady Gwendolen is entitled to read, one way or the other.

We must therefore define receivedNotice to add such a clause to any query that we wish to restrict in this way. You will notice that, unlike the other restrictions we have applied, this one incorporates the name of the join table, `notices_readers`, and the foreign key, `notice_id`. To accommodate general restrictions of this type, we need to parameterize the function exported by the `authorization_filters` module. Rather than pass all the relevant names into the module, we will adopt a convention that when the records for a resource are stored in a table called *rsrcs*, the join table listing the ids of users who can access that resource is called *rsrc*_readers and the foreign key will be *rsrc*_id. That way, only the common prefix needs to be passed to the module.

Listing 20 shows this modification to the module's interface, and the definition of a new method, `whereReader`, which constructs the necessary SQL clause in the form required by the middleware methods which will be called after it. The body of the method just builds the necessary sub-string, and then follows the pattern we showed earlier of assigning to the relevant properties of the request object.

The method `receivedNotice` which, as we described earlier, we need to include in the arrays of route middleware `restrictToReceivedNotices` and `restrictToReceivedNotice`, is `noticeAuthorization.whereReader`, where `noticeAuthorization` is the object returned by passing the string `'notice'` as the argument when we require the `authorization_filters` module.

Providing a suitable interface for the club members to add a list of recipients to some of their notices presents some problems, but they are not relevant to the security aspect of the application, so we will pass over them in silence. We have just assumed that it is somehow possible to create the necessary records in the `notices_readers` table. (In fact, if you download the sample code you will see that we require the recipients' ids to be specified, which is hardly an acceptably user-friendly approach. Something like a text field, auto-completed with names from the `users` table, would be more appropriate.)

Our authorization scheme based on the list of members who may read each notice is an example of the use of an ***access control list (ACL).***

Listing 20

```
1  module.exports = function(tablePrefix) {
2
3    var table = tablePrefix + 's';
4    var joinTable = table + '_readers';
5    var key = tablePrefix + '_id';
6
7    return {
8
9  //   allResources, whereId, whereUser as before
10
11     whereReader: function(req, res, next) {
12       var queryString1 = 'not exists (select * from ' + joinTable +
13                          ' where ' + key + ' = ' + table + '.id)';
14       var queryString2 = 'id in (select ' + key + ' from ' +
15                          joinTable + ' where user_id = ?)';
16       var queryString = '(' + queryString1 + ' or '
17                          + queryString2 + ')';
18       req.dbQuery = req.dbQuery?
19                     req.dbQuery + ' and ' + queryString:
20                     queryString;
21       req.dbQueryValues.push(req.userId);
22       next()
23     }
24   }
25 }
```

In general, an ACL associates a list of users with a resource, with the users on the list being those who are authorized to perform some operation on that resource. For instance, if it made sense to allow certain users of the application to update a notice, we could construct ACLs in the form of a table called notices_writers. We would use this table in a middleware method to restrict the result of SQL queries to records corresponding to notices that the current user was allowed to update. This middleware could then be used in any route for a controller action that led to a notice's being updated.

ACLs can be as specific as necessary. Their established use in operating systems, and the ubiquity of CRUD database operations in Web applications, suggests using ACLs for controlling reading, writing and deleting resources. (Creation is a problematic case, because at the time of creation, there is no resource with which to associate the ACL. In Unix-like operating systems, this problem is solved by noting that creating a file is the same as writing an entry to a directory, but this trick is not always available for other types of resource.)

There is no reason for ACLs to be confined to these operations, though. If you can identify an operation on a resource that you need to restrict to a set of authorized users, and you have a mechanism for building ACLs that specify the set of users who can perform that operation, you can implement the authorization by consulting the ACL. Generalizing the middleware to accommodate arbitrary ACLs is left as an exercise for interested readers.

Key Points

- HTTP requests are the only way in which users and programs can invoke operations that create, retrieve, update or destroy resources managed by a Web application.

- Authorization consists of determining whether it is permissible for the current user to perform the action invoked by an incoming request on the resource which the request refers to.

- If each resource has an owner, it may be appropriate to allow certain operations on a resource to be performed only by its owner.

- An application that maintains user accounts needs to ensure that a user's account can only be modified or destroyed by its owner (or an administrator).

- If a user is treated as a singular resource, according to the conventions of REST, URLs will never specify a user id, and all requests can be applied to the current user's data.

- Identifying the restricted routes and applying the authentication middleware is all that is necessary to implement authorization for actions on users' accounts, because the currentUser method makes only the authorized data available to the actions.

- If each resource has a single owner and a user may own several resources, there is a one-to-many relationship between users and resources, which can be modelled in a relational database by including the user id as a foreign key in the records for the resources.

- In Express, an array of middleware can be applied to requests sent to URLs matching a regular expression.

- Authentication and authorization can be applied to URLs sharing a common prefix by applying a suitable middleware array to a route that matches all such URLs.

- A useful pattern consists of authentication, which also retrieves the current user's id, followed by a sequence of methods that builds a query to retrieve one or more resources, subject to any relevant authorization restrictions, followed by a method that executes the query. Partial queries and the retrieved data can be passed in the request object.

- To ensure that users can only perform operations on resources they own, the middleware array can be used to build a query that only retrieves resource records whose user_id foreign key matches the current user's id. Only authorized data will be passed to the controller, which therefore does not need to perform any checks of its own.

- When authorization constraints depend on a many-to-many relationship, a join table containing keys for the resource and user must be maintained.

- The middleware array must then build and execute a query that uses the join table to ensure that the constraints are satisfied.

- An access control list (ACL) associates a list of users with a resource, with the users on the list being those who are authorized to perform some operation on that resource.

- If an operation on a resource needs to be restricted to a set of authorized users, the authorization can be implemented by consulting an ACL that specifies the list of users who may perform that operation.

Role-Based Authorization

Restricting operations on resources to those invoked by requests sent by their owners is a common pattern of authorization, but it is not the only one. We have mentioned in passing the need to have administrators with access to all resources. In many situations it is also necessary to define different classes of user with different levels of access to resources. It is customary to identify the class a user belongs to by assigning each user a *role*, which determines the operations they are authorized to perform. For example, "administrator" is a role in any application that accords special privileges to some users for administering the application; "premium subscriber" might be a role in an application that offered different levels of service depending on the level of subscription a customer paid. Roles reflect not only the services provided by the application, but also properties of its users in the real world, such as whether they are employed to administer it, or pay to use it.

Further generalizing our technique of applying authorization restrictions using a combination of URLs and route middleware to accommodate these more elaborate situations is not difficult.

Administrators

In many cases, it is only necessary to distinguish two roles. Ordinary users all have the same set of privileges. Usually there are no restrictions on what users can do to their own resources, but they can only perform limited operations on other users' resources, at most being allowed read access to them. Distinguished administrators, or more colloquially, admin users, can perform most operations on any users' resources. Putting it another way, admin users are permitted to request certain operations that must be denied to ordinary users.

Our use of URL prefixes to group together a set of routes to which some middleware must be applied is well suited to restricting certain operations to admin users.

> ## Obscure URLs
>
> Even the most dim-witted aspiring hacker will realize that URL paths beginning /admin are likely to offer ways in to a privileged interface. Choosing a different path prefix, such as /mission_control doesn't provide any real extra security: your admin interface ought to be thoroughly secure anyway, and a determined skilled attacker will discover the actual path eventually. However, amateur hackers will never look beyond /admin, so you will gain some comfort from not seeing so many unauthorized attempts to log in as an admin user in your application's logs. It is conceivable that you will gain some protection against the consequences of weak passwords this way, although you should never be using weak admin passwords.

If we include a route such as

```
app.all('/admin/:resource/:id?/:op?', restrictToAdministrator);
```

then we can use RESTful URLs with the prefix /admin for any requests that access a resource in a way that is only permitted to admin users, provided we can define a suitable filter restrictToAdministrator, which ensures that only requests send by admin users will be accepted for these routes.

For instance, one of the things admin users almost always need to be able to do is forcibly delete the accounts of users who misbehave. Sometimes, an admin user needs to be able to edit other users' accounts. (We will show an example later.) Earlier, we treated the current user's account as a singular resource to prevent an ordinary user accessing others' accounts. From the admin user's point of view, user accounts constitute a resource which is not singular, as in Table 1. It should be possible for the admin user to see a list of all accounts, and select an account to view, edit or delete, by including an id in a URL. In some applications, the creation of user accounts is reserved to the admin user, but in our application we allow users to create their own accounts, and do not allow the admin user to do so.

These administrative operations on user accounts must be performed in a separate controller from the one that we showed you earlier, which allows users to administer their own accounts. If we assign the object exported from a suitable administrators' controller to userRecordsController, we can define routes as follows:

```
app.get ('/admin/users', allowAnyUsers, userRecordsController.
index);
app.get ('/admin/users/:id', allowAnyUser, userRecordsController.
show);
app.get ('/admin/users/:id/edit', allowAnyUser,
userRecordsController.edit);
app.put ('/admin/users/:id', allowAnyUser, userRecordsController.
update);
app.del ('/admin/users/:id', allowAnyUser, userRecordsController.
destroy);
```

The two middleware arrays used here, allowAnyUsers and allowAnyUser, employ the strategy we developed earlier for selecting and loading records from the users table. As the names imply, they do not impose any restrictions on the User objects that are selected. This is correct, because all these routes are prefixed with /admin, so the general route for admin URLs will match them first, causing any requests that are not sent by the admin user to be rejected. Using this approach, simply prefixing a URL with /admin is enough to impose the authorization requirement, provided the general route appears before any others that match the URL. Being able to separate the authorization in this way has allowed us to re-use the middleware for selecting and loading resources without being concerned about whether the operations are permissible.

The array restrictToAdministrator could comprise the following methods:

```
[restrictToAuthenticated, loadCurrentUser, adminOnly]
```

The first two of these are the same as those we used for any user, since an admin user is normally a user too. It is the last method, adminOnly, which is used to reject any requests that don't come from admin users. Its definition depends on how we distinguish our admin users. There are several possible ways of doing this.

If there is to be only one admin user, a simple way of identifying them is by using a distinguished name: admin is a popular choice, but if you think that offers too obvious a target for brute force attackers, you can choose any other name you like, such as manager or guvnor, or even a random string of characters. If users must sign up with their email addresses, the admin user could have a name that was not a syntactically valid email address. This ensures that it is not possible for anybody to create the admin user's account by misappropriating the normal sign-up process – for example, by connecting to the application immediately after it has been deployed, before the real admin user has been created. (At that point, the bogus admin user would be detected and presumably deleted, but depending on the application, there may have been an opportunity in the meantime to plant some "back door" for illicit access.)

It is almost always necessary to create the admin user by some means outside the normal behaviour of the application. For example, in the present case, you could create a record in the users table for admin by way of the database's command line tools. Alternatively a special setup script could be supplied that was run when the application was deployed. In that case, the setup script should be deleted, preferably automatically, as soon as it has run. You must also ensure that the application cannot accept requests until an admin user has been created.

It should go without saying that the admin user's password must be a hard one. It is stupid to set up the admin user with a default password, because system administrators too often leave the default in place, and as we remarked in the chapter about *Accounts*, default passwords soon become widely known. Instead, if a script is used to set up the admin account, it must require the password to be set, and should probably use a password strength checker to reject insecure passwords.

If the admin user is identified by their name, defining adminOnly is just a matter of checking whether the current user's name is admin (or whichever name has been chosen). To be precise, the method needs to test whether req.currentUser.emailAddress is equal to 'admin', even though this user is not identified by an actual email address. Although this is not a real shortcoming of the scheme, it does suggest that something is not quite right: we are using a field supposed to serve as an identifier for the user to determine whether they are an admin user.

A cleaner alternative is to allow the admin user to be identified by their email address, like any other user, and to use some other means of marking them as an administrator.

The solution that probably suggests itself to many programmers, of adding a Boolean flag called something like is_admin to the records in the users table, is not recommended. You might use a flag of this sort if you were creating objects in memory, but it is inefficient in a database. Instead, the usual way of recording membership of a set in a relational database (which is what we need to do) is by creating a separate table, possibly called administrators, with a single field containing a user id value, and adding the key of the admin user's record in the users table to it. You can see that this gives us an immediate bonus: we can have more than one admin user.

Listing 21

```
1 User.prototype.checkAdmin = function(callback) {
2   var self = this;
3   db.fetchRow('select * from admins where user_id = ?',
4     self.id, function(err, u) {
5       callback(!err && u);
6   });
7 };
```

Listing 22

```
1  module.exports = {
2    restrictToAdmin: function(req, res, next) {
3      req.currentUser.checkAdmin(function(isAdmin) {
4        if (isAdmin)
5          next();
6        else
7          res.render('forbidden', {status: 403,
8                          message: 'Forbidden',
9                          title: 'Access Forbidden',
10                         layout: 'blank-layout'});
11     })
12   }
```

The drawback is that we now need to perform a database operation to determine whether the current user is an admin user. One way of arranging matters is by adding a method to the User model, which tries to retrieve a record from the admins table and passes a Boolean value to a callback to indicate whether it was successful in doing so. Listing 21 shows how this can be implemented, while Listing 22 shows how it can be used to define a suitable authorization method. If the object exported from the module in Listing 22 is assigned to a variable roleAuthorization, the adminOnly middleware that we need is just roleAuthorization.restrictToAdmin.

In the next section we will show a further refinement of this approach.

We have implicitly assumed that when the admin user logs in, they do so using the same login form as any other user. This serves to authenticate them, which means that the application can recognize them as an admin user, in the fashion just described. Where the integrity of an application's data is considered especially important, it is possible, and may be considered desirable, to use a separate logging-in mechanism for admin users. The simple way to arrange this is by providing a URL such as /adminlogin, routed to a modified version of the login controller. This could require additional authentication, or be restricted to certain nominated IP addresses. The ordinary login page would then have to reject login attempts using an admin user's email address. Alternatively, the standard login procedure could be used, but if it was determined that the user logging in was an admin user, some additional verification could be called for.

If the admin user does not need to have an ordinary user's account, and only performs administrative functions that are denied to other users, it may be possible to separate admin users from all other users and deal with them independently. That is, admin passwords could be stored in a different table from other users' passwords, or possibly not even be stored in the database at all. You might consider using HTTP authentication for admin users when session-based authentication is being used for everybody else. That way, any successful attack on the database would not automatically provide attackers with admin access.

If you take such an approach, it is essential that you provide a means for admin users to change their passwords as easily as any other user can. Don't, for example, hard code a hash of the admin password in the source code of the application. If the password is compromised, the first thing that should be done is change it. If there is no simple way to do this, there may be no alternative to closing down the application. The application's administrators may not be its developers, so if it is necessary to edit source code to change the password, it may be some time before the change could be made.

What ought to happen if the admin user's password is forgotten? As we explained when considering user accounts, resetting a password is always a slightly perilous procedure, and the relatively secure method we described in the chapter on *Accounts* relies on the assumption that a user's email is confidential. You cannot assume that the admin password will never be forgotten, especially if it's a string of random characters. Equally, you cannot assume that keeping the password written down in "a secure place" will keep it safe. You must always allow for the possibility of its being forgotten. If you do not think that sending a password reset token to a specified email address is sufficiently safe, you will have to provide a special script for resetting the admin password, that is not part of the application proper. If it is feasible, you can restrict the running of this script to a designated IP address or, if you have physical access to the server, only allow it to be run from the console.

Roles

Sometimes it is enough to distinguish between admin users and all other users, but often there are more distinctions to be made between different classes of user of an application. For instance, it is very common for Web-based services to provide different levels of facilities, depending on the "plan" chosen – in other words, the size of the subscription paid. A free plan will offer a limited introduction to the service, a basic plan will be adequate for individuals with modest needs, a premium plan will include extra services, an enterprise plan will allow for intensive use, and so on. Authorization is needed to ensure that users can only use the facilities that they have paid for.

Conceivably, ACLs could be used to implement this type of authorization. Lists of the users subscribing to each plan could be maintained in the database and associated with resources and operations, in the way we used the list of recipients to restrict access to notices. These lists would become unwieldy and hard to maintain as the number of users increased. The more conventional alternative is to assign each user a role, chosen from a set of roles that correspond to the different classes of user. Authorization is then performed by specifying a set of roles that may access a resource using a certain operation.

At an abstract level, the two strategies are the same. We are grouping users into sets, and restricting certain operations on some resources to members of one or more of these sets. ACLs contain the members of the sets themselves; roles stand in for the sets.

It is not difficult to implement authorization based on roles, using the ideas we have described in the preceding sections.

First, we need a way of representing the relationship between users and their roles. Every user normally only plays one role, so there is a one-to-many relationship, which could be represented by creating a `roles` table containing an id and usually a role name, and adding a `role_id` foreign key to the `users` table. Often, though not always, roles are hierarchical, however. That is, if Abelardo's tiddlywinks club went commercial and offered premium and enterprise plans as well as the basic service, an enterprise user would be able to do everything a premium user could and more, while a premium user could do everything a basic user could and more. This suggests that each role should be given a numerical level, such that if a user with role R has more privileges than a user with role S, and R and S have been given the levels r and s, $r > s$. In a situation where admin users are users with exceptional privileges, so that they can perform any operation available to any other user as well as some additional operations, admin authorization is trivially incorporated by defining an admin role at a level higher than any other role. There is no need for a separate `administrators` table.

It is sensible to allocate non-contiguous values for roles, in case the need ever arises for defining a new role in between two old ones. For Abelardo's tiddlywinks club, we defined constants for the role levels as follows:

```
var BASIC = 0, PREMIUM = 10, ENTERPRISE = 20, ADMIN = 999;
```

If this scheme is adopted, there is no real need for an explicit roles table. Instead of adding a role id to each user's record, we add their role level. The `roles` table might be retained to record names for each role, if it was necessary to display these, or it might be combined with, for example, a table describing each plan and storing its subscription rate. However, it no longer needs to play a part in authorization.

Listing 23 shows a module that exports a simple function for generating authentication middleware based on role levels. The filtering mechanism itself is trivial: it just compares the level of the current user's role with the value originally passed as the argument to `restrictToRole`. Given the

Listing 23

```
1  module.exports = {
2    restrictToRole: function(level) {
3      return function(req, res, next) {
4        if (req.currentUser.roleLevel >= level)
5          next();
6        else
7          res.render('forbidden', {status: 403,
8                          message: 'Forbidden',
9                          title: 'Access Forbidden',
10                         layout: 'blank-layout'});
11
12     };
13   }
14 }
```

constants shown above, we would construct a collection of authentication methods in the following way:

```
var roleAuthorization =
      require('./middleware/authorization_by_role'),
  adminOnly = roleAuthorization.restrictToRole(ADMIN),
  enterpriseOnly=roleAuthorization.restrictToRole(ENTERPRISE),
  premiumOnly = roleAuthorization.restrictToRole(PREMIUM);
```

Our previous version of adminOnly has been neatly subsumed under this new scheme.

The rest should be routine by now. The methods just defined can be incorporated in route middleware arrays that perform authorization, as we have done before. With our set of roles, these would be as shown in Listing 24.

As a trivial example of the application of this authorization middleware, suppose that members who pay for a premium-level membership get the privilege of creating an individualized signature to append to their notices.

Listing 24

```
 1  var restrictToAuthenticatedUser =
 2      [restrictToAuthenticated, loadCurrentUser];
 3  var restrictToPremiumUser =
 4      [restrictToAuthenticated, loadCurrentUser,
 5        premiumOnly];
 6  var restrictToEnterpriseUser =
 7      [restrictToAuthenticated, loadCurrentUser,
 8        enterpriseOnly];
 9  var restrictToAdministrator =
10      [restrictToAuthenticated, loadCurrentUser,
11        adminOnly];
```

Enterprise users can create signatures too. They can also see a list of all the club's members and read any member's profile (because that's the sort of thing enterprise users like to be able to do). Admin users have all these privileges, and they can also delete any user's account. We will assume that administrators can change users' roles, though it is often the case that if a role depends on the payment of a fee, it will be changed automatically when payment is received. (This is a special case that we will not consider here.) Obviously, users cannot change their own roles by any other means, though they must still be able to change their email addresses and passwords.

Listing 25 shows the routes that must be defined to allow users of each type to perform the operations they are entitled to and no others. We create routes that catch all requests to URLs with a certain prefix and apply appropriate middleware to restrict them to users at the appropriate role level. Then we create routes for each operation, suitably prefixed, and incorporating any additional middleware needed to load the resource or resources which the requests refer to.

Only two points require further comment. Since some users need to be able to access their signatures, we have created a signatures table and defined a method called loadUserSignature to perform a simple database lookup that attaches the signature to the request. As it introduces no new ideas, we will not show the details. This method is added to routes that access

Listing 25

```
 1  app.all('/user/:resource/:id?/:op?',
 2    restrictToAuthenticatedUser);
 3  app.get ('/user/notices/new', noticesController.new);
 4  app.post('/user/notices', noticesController.create);
 5  app.get ('/user/notices', restrictToReceivedNotices,
 6    noticesController.index);
 7  app.get ('/user/notices/:id', restrictToReceivedNotice,
 8    noticesController.show);
 9  app.get ('/user/notices/:id/edit', restrictToOwnersNotice,
10    noticesController.edit);
11  app.put ('/user/notices/:id', restrictToOwnersNotice,
12    noticesController.update);
13  app.del ('/user/notices/:id', restrictToOwnersNotice,
14    noticesController.destroy);
15
16  app.all('/premium/:resource/:id?/:op?',
17    restrictToPremiumUser);
18  app.get ('/premium/signature', loadUserSignature,
19    sigController.show);
20  app.get ('/premium/signature/new', sigController.new);
21  app.post('/premium/signature', sigController.create);
22  app.get ('/premium/signature/edit', loadUserSignature,
23    sigController.edit);
24  app.put ('/premium/signature', loadUserSignature,
25    sigController.update);
26  app.del ('/premium/signature', loadUserSignature,
27    sigController.destroy);
28
29  app.all('/enterprise/:resource/:id?/:op?',
30    restrictToEnterpriseUser);
31  app.get ('/enterprise/users', allowAnyUsers,
32    userRecordsController.index);
33  app.get ('/enterprise/users/:id', allowAnyUser,
34    userRecordsController.show);
35
36  app.all('/admin/:resource/:id?/:op?',
37    restrictToAdministrator);
38  app.get ('/admin/users/:id/edit', allowAnyUser,
39    userRecordsController.edit);
40  app.put ('/admin/users/:id', allowAnyUser,
41    userRecordsController.update);
42  app.del ('/admin/users/:id', allowAnyUser,
43    userRecordsController.destroy);
```

the methods from a controller for performing operations on signature resources. Again, since this controller is entirely routine, we will not show it here.

All the routes for URLs beginning with the prefixes /admin/users and /enterprise/users invoke methods in the controller that is referred to in the routes as userRecordsController. As before, this is separate from the userController that is invoked when users edit their own profiles. In these restricted routes, users are considered plural resources.

You should be able to see how the authorization scheme we have outlined could be applied to any number of roles, providing they are hierarchically arranged, so that users at each level are authorized to perform all the operations authorized for lower levels plus some additional ones. Such an arrangement often occurs naturally when users are offered a range of plans for the various services on offer.

Sometimes, the relationship between roles may not be strictly hierarchical, but other arrangements can easily be accommodated. The authorization middleware just has to consult a list of roles instead of comparing the current user's role's level with a threshold.

A more interesting case arises when authorization depends not just on the user's role, but also on the particular resource they are accessing.

Consider, as an example, another of Abelardo's businesses – his project hosting service CodePot. Developers can sign up to the service and create projects, each of which has its own code repository, issue tracking pages, documentation collection, and so on. Each project will also have its own manager and a collection of developers working on the project at any time. Access may also be granted to visitors, so they can learn about the project and its progress.

This suggests that Abelardo's CodePot needs at least five classes of user. Abelardo himself is a superuser, with powers to make any changes to the

Authorizing Views

Every user must be provided with a means of sending requests for every operation which they are entitled to perform, which may depend on their role. The views rendered by the controller provide the normal interface to an application, and since these are HTML documents, they need to include links or buttons for sending requests. Usually, therefore, the set of links and buttons displayed on a page depends on the current user's role.

For example, suppose that the tiddlywinks club's site we have been describing has a main navbar, which is displayed on every page and contains links to each section of the site which a user is entitled to visit. An enterprise user would see links labelled Notices, leading to a list of all the notices they could read, Settings, leading to the form for changing their account details, Signature, since every enterprise user is also a premium user and has access to the form to change a signature, and Users, to see the list of all users. However, a basic user cannot create or edit a signature, nor see a list of all users. Ideally, therefore, they should not see the Signature or Users links.

It is simple to determine which links should be displayed by inspecting the current user's role. You could consider this a case of authorization being applied to views, but it provides no real security, since attackers can always manufacture requests without using the site's pages. Conversely, failing to filter out the inappropriate links is not a serious security flaw. All that will happen is that for some users, clicking on a navbar link will cause a response with a status code of 404 (not found) or 403 (forbidden) to be returned, instead of the requested resource. Including links to forbidden operations does provide attackers with extra information about the application's URL structure, but usability considerations should already be sufficient motivation for not displaying these links.

system and to administer the accounts of anybody who signs up. Then there are administrators, who represent an organization that has signed up to use the service. Administrators can create new projects and close old ones. Each project has a manager, who can manage the project's repositories, and is appointed by an administrator. Within a project, there must be developers, who do the work and may upload files. Finally, visitors are a separate category, who only have read access to repositories.

Each category of user can be given a role. The roles can be assigned levels to restrict their capabilities. An ACL can be associated with each project to list the developers working on that project. The manager of a project can be treated as its owner, after it has been created by an administrator. Thus, all the restrictions appropriate to this application can be implemented using a combination of the techniques we have described so far.

The tools we have developed in the preceding sections provide considerable power and flexibility for implementing different authorization strategies. However, specifying the restrictions for a complex application with many roles is repetitive work, and care must be taken to ensure that the restrictions on each route are specified correctly. The likely response of most programmers to this situation is to abstract the common pattern and provide a higher-level interface, probably in the form of a domain-specific language (DSL), to the specification of authorization constraints. Authorization extensions of this sort are common in mature frameworks such as Ruby on Rails (notably the CanCan gem) and Django (Django-Guardian). At the time of writing, there is no equivalent for use in Express applications.

It's easy to get carried away once you have the power of such a system at your disposal. Complexity always brings the potential for errors, and simple systems are usually easier to secure than complex ones. If an authorization scheme that does no more than distinguish between administrators and other users is adequate for your needs, you should use it.

Model-Based Authorization

We have concentrated on the use of route middleware to apply authorization to requests, but it is also possible to apply authorization to operations on models. That is, instead of checking whether a request is trying to access resources which perhaps should be denied to it, the application waits until an attempt is made to access data through a model and performs the check then. ACLs and roles can be used to determine which users may perform each available operation on a particular model. (For instance, an admin user can edit any User object.) Any restrictions can be enforced by inserting a filter method before any method defined in a model that is subject to authorization.

Since a model should be the only way to access persistent data, placing the access controls in the model protects the data from all unauthorized access, no matter where the model operations were invoked from. In a well-written Web application, model operations should only ever be invoked from controllers, so applying authorization to requests ought to provide all the protection that is necessary. Model-based authorization is only useful in preventing unauthorized operations on data that have been invoked as a result of attacks that circumvent the controller. Other methods can and should be adopted to prevent such attacks, but many security experts advocate a strategy of "defence in depth", which means that redundant security mechanisms should be deployed in case one or more of them succumbs to an attacker. Authorizing both requests and model operations provides such redundancy, if it is felt to be required. There is a performance penalty, because additional database accesses will be required by the extra checks.

Note, also, that the model-based approach does not provide any way of enforcing authorization on other operations, such as the sending of email messages.

Key Points

- It is often necessary to define roles that assign different levels of access to resources.

- Each user's role determines the operations they are authorized to perform.

- In many cases, there are only two roles: ordinary users and administrators.

- Using a common prefix for all URLs that invoke operations that should be restricted to administrators allows authorization middleware to be used to impose the restrictions.

- Defining a filter which ensures that only requests send by administrators will be accepted for these routes is enough to secure the admin interface.

- If there is only one administrator, a simple way of identifying them is by using a distinguished name, such as admin, or a special email address.

- Alternatively, administrators may have accounts like other users, and a table containing the ids of users records for administrators can be used to identify them for the purpose of authorization. This scheme allows several users to be administrators.

- Always ensure that it is possible to change the administrator's password. Do not embed it into the code.

- Where possible, take extra precautions when an administrator's password needs to be reset if it has been forgotten.

- If more distinctions must be made between different classes of user of an application, each user can be assigned a role, and authorization can be performed by specifying a set of roles that may access a resource using a certain operation.

- A user's role may be specified by recording a role id, identifying a row in a roles table, as a foreign key in the users table.

- If the roles define a strict hierarchy of privilege, it is sufficient to assign each role a level, and record a role level for each user.

- Authorization middleware can be applied to each route to restrict the corresponding action to users with roles at or above a specific level.

- If roles do not form a hierarchy, the authorization middleware must consult a list of roles specifying those which are permitted to perform the operation.

- Routes restricted to the same roles can be grouped together with a common path prefix, and the authorization middleware can be applied to the whole group.

- For complex applications, it may be necessary to combine role-based authorization with ACLs.

OAuth

A prominent feature of modern Web applications is the sharing of information by way of Web APIs. Web applications may exchange data between themselves instead of sending it to a browser.

For example, many developers have accounts at the code-sharing site Github, so it is reasonable for CodePot, Abelardo's project hosting service, to provide its users with access to their Github profiles and repositories. That way, their contact details can be synchronized between the two sites, and it will be fairly easy to import or export code. Github restricts operations on profiles and repositories, so if a developer wants to update their email address, for example, they must be logged in. If Github has only implemented authentication and authorization by the methods we have described so far in this book, the only way a developer such as Abelardo's associate Zak could arrange for CodePot to interact with Github would be by storing his Github password on the CodePot site.

Sharing a password always compromises security. The security afforded by passwords depends on their not being shared. Sharing a password with a third party whose trustworthiness is unknown is obviously undesirable.

Even if the honesty of the site's operators is unimpeachable, as in the case of Abelardo, so that a third party might safely be trusted with a password, there remains a compelling reason for not doing so. In order to log in to Github, a request including Zak's credentials must be sent. CodePot can only do this if it stores his password in plain text (or encrypted using some reversible algorithm). By now, you should realize that this is something that no Web site should ever do, so some other means of authorizing Web applications is essential.

OAuth is a protocol (more properly, a protocol framework) that attempts to facilitate such interactions between applications in a properly secure manner. From the user's point of view, OAuth is similar to OpenId, as described in the chapter on *Authentication*. In the scenario just outlined,

Zak might change the email address recorded in his profile while he was logged in at codepot.com.fd. On the profile page there would be an option to export the changes to Github. When he clicked the button to do so, he would be redirected to Github, where he would be asked to log in, then shown a dialogue explaining that codepot.com.fd had requested access to his profile. If he agreed to grant that access he would be redirected back to codepot.com.fd, where the exporting takes place.

Behind the scenes, however, OAuth and OpenId are doing different things. Whereas OpenId just checks the user's identity and sends back a response confirming it, OAuth sends back a token. This token can be used in subsequent requests almost as a substitute for a valid user session (which, as we explained earlier, is itself a substitute for a password), to allow access to restricted resources. Usually, the token does not provide unrestricted access, and its validity may be limited to a short time, often just an hour or two. Before it can even ask for the token, the site that is requesting access must authenticate itself to the site providing it, so there is a double authentication: first the site identifies itself, then the customer identifies himself. After this double authentication, authorization based on the token that was obtained is used in every request for data.

The basic idea behind OAuth authorization is thus fairly simple, but in order to implement it securely, steps must be taken to ensure that tokens cannot be intercepted, faked or obtained under false pretences. These requirements add considerably to the protocol's complexity.

Originally, OAuth depended on an exchange of public keys between the sites when the sharing arrangement is first set up, to allow the subsequent interactions to be done over a secure connection. When all the necessary key and token exchanges are taken into account, authorization using OAuth 1.0 ends up as a complicated interaction, which is difficult to implement correctly. In an attempt to make it easier, a somewhat simplified version, known as OAuth WRAP (Web Resource Authorization Protocol) was defined. The main simplification was to require the use of HTTPS, which renders the key exchange required by OAuth 1.0 redundant, at the expense of making it impossible for sites that do not use HTTPS to provide OAuth authorization. OAuth WRAP served as the basis of a new version 2.0 of OAuth, which is being prepared by the IETF.

Github provides a well-documented example of a Web API protected by OAuth 2. We can use it to illustrate the steps that a site must take to obtain authorized access to data from another site. (The details below are accurate at the time of writing, but we cannot guarantee that Github will not make changes to the interface in the future.)

Before his site can be authorized to access users' profiles and repositories, Abelardo must register CodePot at Github, by providing its name, its URL, and a second URL, known as the *redirection endpoint*, which will be used as the destination of HTTP redirects during OAuth exchanges between the application and Github. Abelardo must register his site manually, by filling in a simple form while he is logged in at Github. Each registered application is assigned a unique Client ID and a value known as the Client Secret. These values are used to authenticate the application when it communicates with Github's API.

When Zak tries to access his profile from Abelardo's project hosting site, his browser is redirected by CodePot sending a response with status code of 301, and the URL in the Location header set to https://github.com/login/oauth/authorize, Github's *authorization endpoint*. Note that this is an HTTPS URL, so the resulting GET request and its response will be encrypted, and the identity of the Github site will be verified. A query string is appended to the URL to send some parameters in the request. These must include the Client ID (as a parameter called client_id). The query string should also include a parameter called state, whose value is a random string generated by the application. Optionally, the request also includes a URL to which Zak's browser will be redirected after interacting with Github. If this URL is omitted, the redirection endpoint URL provided when the application was registered is used. The query string may also include a parameter called scope, which comprises a list of code names for the different types of access being requested.

The permissible values are determined by the server providing the authorization. For example, in the case of Github the user scope requests read/write access to profiles only, whereas the public_repo scope requests access to public repositories, and the repo scope requests access to public and private repositories. Since CodePot needs access to users' profiles and their public repositories, the value of the scope parameter in the query string would be user, public_repo.

When the request for the authorization endpoint is received, Zak is prompted to log in to Github (if he isn't already logged in there). If he has already given CodePot the permissions to access Github specified in the request, he is immediately redirected back to the redirection endpoint (or the URL specified in the request). Otherwise, Github displays a dialogue informing Zak that CodePot has requested access to his profile and public repositories, and asking him to confirm that he wishes to allow this access. If he agrees, he is redirected. The URL in the redirection has two parameters, the state as sent in the request, and a temporary code, sent as the value of the code parameter.

After Zak's browser receives the redirect response from Github it sends a GET request to the URL, including the parameters in the query string, in the Location header. The CodePot site checks the value of the state, to ensure that it has genuinely been sent in response to the original request. If so, a POST request is sent to Github. The body of this request includes the Client ID and Client Secret, to verify that it is being sent by the application registered with Github, the state value again, to show that the message is part of the same exchange, and the code just received from Github.

The response to this request will include a unique *access token*. The format of this token is not specified by the OAuth specification, but it will appear to be a random string. Whenever a call is made to Github's API, the access token must be included as a parameter. For instance, to retrieve Zak's profile data, the request

```
GET https://api.github.com/user?access_token=e72e16c7e42f292c69
12e7710c838347ae178b4a
```

would be sent, where the long string beginning e72... was the access code retrieved by the earlier step. The data will only be returned if the access code is valid for the operation being requested.

The scope of OAuth 2.0 extends beyond the sort of data exchange between Web sites that we have described. It can also be applied to authorizing mobile and desktop clients to access restricted resources, and to authorization performed by client-side scripts without an intervening server application.

An increasingly common requirement that is addressed by OAuth is for users to be able to share data about themselves between their personal profiles on different social networking sites. Instead of entering all the relevant information on each new site they join, some people would prefer to be able to import their profile from a site that already holds their information. Almost always, this information includes an email address. Retrieving a user's email address using OAuth provides a means of authenticating that user. This method of authentication lies behind popular options for logging in to third-party sites using credentials registered at Facebook, Twitter or other popular sites that maintain user profiles.

Abelardo could allow developers to log in to CodePot using their Github credentials. If Zak tried to login to the CodePot site by clicking on the login link, he would be redirected to Github's authorization endpoint URL, as described above, with the scope parameter set to user. As a result, he would be required to authenticate himself at Github. If, after the OAuth setup was completed, Abelardo's site requested Zak's profile data, using the access token received, the email address included in the response must belong to Zak, since only he could authorize Github to provide the profile. Thus, Abelardo does not need to store a password for Zak at CodePot, because he can rely on Github to handle that. The CodePot application only needs to verify that Zak is a registered user.

Unfortunately, Abelardo can only avoid maintaining a password-based authentication system entirely if he is prepared to insist that all users of his service have Github accounts. Using OAuth authorization as a way of performing authentication necessarily means that users are required to store credentials with some other site – in the real world this is usually Facebook, Google or Twitter. Many people are understandably reluctant to be forced to sign up with one of these companies, whose own record on security is patchy, and whose attitude to the privacy of their users' data is often lamentable. Hence, using OAuth for logins only offers some convenience to some users. It is not a substitute for password-based authentication for most sites.

If you do decide to allow users to log in to your site with their credentials from some other site that uses OAuth to authorize the export of profile data, you will find that there are minor differences in the precise details of the OAuth implementations. For example, Github's documentation specifies that the access token be requested using POST, but Facebook specifies using GET for that request. Such minor differences are allowed by the OAuth 2.0 standard, which takes an excessively permissive approach to specification. The following extract sums up the problems:

1.8. Interoperability

OAuth 2.0 provides a rich authorization framework with well-defined security properties. However, as a rich and highly extensible framework with many optional components, on its own, this specification is likely to produce a wide range of non-interoperable implementations.

In addition, this specification leaves a few required components partially or fully undefined (e.g. client registration, authorization server capabilities, endpoint discovery). Without these components, clients must be manually and specifically configured against a specific authorization server and resource server in order to interoperate.

To make matters worse, some prominent sites still continue to use OAuth 1, or a revised version known as OAuth 1.0a, which fixes a vulnerability in the original OAuth protocol.

If your concern is with accessing some well-known site via its Web APIs, you will find it most convenient to use a plug-in or middleware for the site in question ("specifically configured against a specific authorization server and resource server", as the OAuth committee might say). Most Web frameworks offer a selection of these. You will probably find there is a suitable multi-purpose authentication plug-in that can be used to allow users to log in with their credentials from some other site, as described earlier. Plug-ins of this type usually provide a way for developers to implement "strategies" (essentially plug-ins to the plug-in) that incorporate any peculiarities of a particular site's implementation.

If you want to provide a Web API to your own site and need to incorporate features that allow users to authorize other sites and applications to access data using the API, you would be foolish to try and implement your own OAuth authorization scheme from scratch, unless you are an experienced security expert. The permissive specification leaves too many details to developers for it to be used as a recipe for a secure implementation. Getting OAuth wrong may have serious consequences for users' data and privacy. Generally, it is safer to allow access by way of an API only to public data, so that authorization is not necessary. In cases where access to private data is necessary, it is sensible to rely on an established and well-tested Open Source implementation in the form of middleware or a plug-in for the framework you are using.

Key Points

- If a Web application provides an API that can be used to retrieve private data, access by other applications must be authorized.

- Users' passwords cannot be used for this purpose, because it would require third-party sites to store passwords as plain text.

- OAuth is a protocol framework that allows interactions between applications to be authorized securely.

- OAuth allows a user to exchange their password for a secure access token, which can safely be entrusted to a third party.

- OAuth 2.0 stipulates the use of HTTPS, so all messages are encrypted.

- If a Web application wishes to access private data from another site that uses OAuth, it must first be registered with that site, by providing a callback URL. In return it will receive two values: a Client ID and a Client Secret. Registration is usually done manually by the client site's developer.

- When the client requires access to private data on behalf of a user, the user is redirected to the site's authorization endpoint.

- The request must include the Client ID as a parameter, and should include a state parameter, which will be used to ensure that subsequent requests are genuine.

- The request may also include a parameter called scope, which comprises a list of code names for the different types of access being requested.

- When the request is received, the user is prompted to log in, if necessary, and then a dialogue is displayed informing them of the access being requested.

- If they agree to authorize access, their browser is redirected to the client site.

- The request includes a temporary code and a copy of the state parameter.

- A new request is then sent, which includes the Client ID and Client Secret and the temporary code.

- The response to this request contains the access token, which must be included in subsequent API requests for protected data.

- OAuth is often used to authorize access to users' profile data on social networks. Retrieving a user's email address from their profile provides a means of authenticating that user.

- This form of authentication requires each user to have an account with an OAuth provider, such as Facebook or Twitter, and this may not always be acceptable.

- The OAuth 2.0 standard is a permissive specification that fails to ensure interoperabilty, so each site's implementation may differ in small details.

- It is advisable to use established implementations of OAuth, especially if you wish to use it for authorization of your own Web API.

Notes On Cryptography

Many aspects of security require information to be concealed from people and programs, except for those who are intended to see it. *Cryptography*, the science of writing in secret code, provides the predominant means of concealment used in computer security. *Encryption* is the process of transforming readable text into an unintelligible form. The original text is referred to as *plaintext*, while the unintelligible form generated by encryption is called the *ciphertext*. Usually, but not always, it is necessary to be able to reverse the process and turn the ciphertext back into plaintext, a process called *decryption*.

The most common use of encryption is to conceal messages or data in transit. In that case, the message is encrypted by the sender and must be decrypted by the recipient. The sender and recipient are called the **principals** in the transmission of the message. The principals may be people, but are often computer programs, such as a Web browser and a server. They may also be hardware devices. A message may have more than one intended recipient.

The purpose of encryption is to conceal the plaintext from everyone except its intended recipient, so decryption of ciphertext by anyone else must not be possible. Encryption algorithms (**ciphers**) take a parameter, known as a **key**, which determines the ciphertext that will be generated from a given plaintext by the cipher. Changing the key leads to a different ciphertext. Decryption can only be done successfully with a key that matches the one used for encryption.

Cryptographic techniques are used when information must be concealed. Those from whom it is concealed wish to break the cipher, that is, they want to be able to decipher ciphertext without a priori knowledge of the key. *Cryptanalysis* is the science of breaking codes. Both cryptanalysis and cryptography were the subject of much research during the second half of the 20th century, leading to powerful techniques of breaking ciphers and the creation of elaborate ciphers to resist them.

The following brief notes provide basic information about the use of cryptographic techniques in computer network and Web application security. For more details, please consult the book *A Web Developer's Guide to Secure Communication* in this series.

Secret-Key Cryptography

Ciphers have been used for millennia, and until relatively recently it was considered to be the case that the keys for encryption and decryption had to be identical. In that case, there is a single key and the cipher is said to be *symmetrical*. Symmetrical ciphers are also known as *shared key* or *secret key* ciphers, because they require that knowledge of the key be shared between the principals and kept secret from everybody else. Usually, one of the principals chooses a key and sends it to the other. This is a major weakness of secret-key ciphers, because we have to assume that communications can be intercepted, otherwise there would be no need for encryption. Hence, the transmission of the key must be performed by some specially secure means, since its interception would render the ciphertext readable to any eavesdropper.

Probably the simplest secret-key ciphers are shift ciphers, in which a message is encrypted by taking each letter in turn and replacing it with the letter that comes a fixed number after it in the alphabet. This fixed number acts as the key. For example, if the key is 2, a is replaced by c, b by d, and so on. If only letters are being encrypted, y is replaced by a and z by b. Decryption can be performed by someone who knows the key by shifting letters in the opposite direction, so a is replaced by y, and so on.

Shift ciphers are trivially easy to break. Modern ciphers work by dividing the data into blocks and shuffling the bits within each block using a function that combines them with bits of a key in a non-linear fashion, using a combination of exchanging bits and replacing values with others according to an apparently random lookup table. The shuffling is iterated many times. Nevertheless, the process can be reversed by anyone who has the key. The length of the key and the size of the blocks determine how effective the encryption is: longer values provide more security.

AES (the Advanced Encryption Standard) is a US Federal Standard cipher which uses keys of 128, 192 or 256 bits in length, depending on the level of security required. It has superseded the older standard *DES (the Data Encryption Standard)*, although a variant of DES, known as *triple DES (3DES)*, is still in use. A popular alternative is the *Blowfish* cipher, which can take keys of any length between 32 and 448 bits.

All the important modern ciphers are supported by the Open Source library *OpenSSL*. OpenSSL wrappers are available for most programming languages.

Cryptographic Hash Functions and MACs

A *cryptographic hash function* maps strings to fixed-length values (hashes) in such a way that reversing the mapping should not be feasible. Furthermore, although the fixed length of the hash implies that there must be pairs of strings that map to the same hash value, it should not be feasible to find two different strings that map to the same hash. This means that if you have stored the hash value of a string, and are presented with a value that claims to be the same string, you can hash the purported string and compare the resulting hash with the stored one to see whether the two strings really are the same. Cryptographic hash functions are essential to secure password storage.

The value computed from a string by a cryptographic hash function is sometimes referred to as a *message digest*, because the hash value concisely summarizes the contents of the original string or message.

Cryptographic hash functions are based on the same principles as modern encryption algorithms.

Well known and secure hash functions include **bcrypt** and the **SHA-2 (Secure Hash Algorithm)** family. **SHA-1** and **MD5** are older functions which, although still in use, are considered to be vulnerable to attacks. The bcrypt algorithm is based on Blowfish, and can be deliberately made to execute slowly to hamper brute-force attacks. SHA-2 is a family of functions, SHA-224, SHA-256, SHA-384 and SHA-512, identified by the length (in bits) of the resulting hash.

Cryptographic hash functions can be used to ensure that messages have not been tampered with. Any change, no matter how small, in the contents of a message will cause it to hash to a different value, so a hash can be added to a message and the recipient can recompute the hash and check whether it matches the original value. If it does, the message is intact. Normally, though, cryptographic hash functions do not use a key, so anybody intercepting the message and altering it could recompute the hash to conceal their changes. Using a secret key as an extra argument to the hashing function prevents this possibility. The value that is computed by a keyed hash function is called a *message authentication code (MAC)*. **HMAC (Keyed-Hash Message Authentication Code)** is a standard construction for computing MACs using a cryptographic hash function, such as SHA-256.

OpenSSL includes implementations of all the important cryptographic hash functions and HMACs.

Public Key Cryptography

If the keys used for encryption and decryption can be different, there is no need for the principals to share a single key. Instead, a key pair, comprising a public key and a private key, can be generated. A message encrypted using the public key can only be decrypted using the private key, and vice versa. Hence, the public key can be freely distributed and used to encrypt messages to the holder of the private key. Nobody else will be able to decrypt them.

Conversely, any messages encrypted with the private key can be sent to holders of the public key. These messages are not confidential, because the public key may be generally known, but if a message can be decrypted successfully, it can only have been encrypted by the holder of the private key, so its authenticity is assured. As a more efficient way of ensuring confidentiality, a *digital signature* can be generated by encrypting a digest of the message with the private key. The recipient can check the authenticity of the message and ensure that it has not been altered by decrypting the signature, computing a digest of the message as received, and comparing the two values.

The earliest algorithms for public key cryptography were devised in the 1970s. *RSA* (named after the initials of the surnames of its inventors Rivest, Shamir and Adleman) uses the product of two large prime numbers to generate a private/public key pair, and its security depends on our current understanding that factorizing this product to retrieve the original primes requires an infeasible amount of time. Advances in quantum computing may defeat the security of RSA encryption, with dire consequences.

The keys for RSA encryption are much longer than those used by secret-key algorithms. It is recommended that keys should be at least 2048 bits long.

RSA encryption is relatively computationally expensive, and decryption is more so.

A significant limitation of RSA encryption is that it can only be used to encrypt messages of the same length as the key. It is therefore common practice in data communication to use RSA to encrypt a secret key, which can then be transmitted and used to encrypt and decrypt messages using a classical algorithm, such as AES.

Key pairs can be generated using an OpenSSL command.

Certificates

A public key can only be used to verify that a message was signed by the principal who claims to have sent it if the public key used by the recipient to decrypt the signature is genuinely the public key that matches the sender's private key. It is possible for somebody to intercept the transmission of the public key and substitute their own, and subsequently intercept and alter messages and sign them with their own private key.

A *public key certificate* is a document consisting of a public key and some information about its owner, digitally signed by a trusted third party known as a *Certification Authority (CA)* to assert its authenticity. In theory, there can be a chain of certificates, allowing the signature on a certificate to be verified by reference to a higher level certificate, and so on, up to a *root certificate*, which can only be verified by some other means. *Publicly trusted CAs'* root certificates are distributed with Web browsers and used by HTTPS to verify the identity of Web sites (see below). Publicly trusted CAs are usually commercial organizations, whose activities are overseen by an industry consortium called the CA/Browser Forum. They are not subject to legal controls (although organizations issuing certificates for some other purposes are, in some some jurisdictions).

The file formats for certificates and procedures for administering them constitute a *public-key infrastructure (PKI)*. *X.509* is the PKI presently used on the Web.

Certificates may be used for code signing, encrypting email messages, protecting traffic to Web sites, and for other purposes. Each type of use has its own type of certificate. Certificates that are used to protect Web sites are associated with named domains. CAs usually charge a fee for issuing certificates. There are three levels of certificate available for use on the Web. *Domain validation certificates* are relatively cheap, and the CA does little more than check that the applicant owns the domain named on the certificate. *Organization validation certificates* require identifying documentation to be submitted. *Extended validation (EV) certificates* are only issued after detailed vetting of the applicant, and only to legally registered businesses or government organizations.

The reliance on organizations which are ultimately self-policing, and certain difficulties with revoking certificates, have led some experts to question the reliability of the X.509 PKI, but it is the only available mechanism for validating public keys used on the Web.

Secure Communication on the Web

Transport Layer Security (TLS) is used on the Internet as a secure protocol for data exchange. It can be used to transport messages in higher-level protocols, especially HTTP, in a secure manner. TLS is a development of an earlier protocol called *Secure Sockets Layer (SSL)*, and the name SSL is still often used instead.

A client and server set up a secure TLS connection using a sequence of messages, the effect of which is that the server sends a public key certificate to the client and then the client uses this to encrypt a random number which it sends to the server. This random number is then used to compute keys for a secret key encryption algorithm, and for computing MACs. The client and server independently generate these keys from the random number sent by the client and various other values known to both parties. The actual sequence of messages is quite elaborate, in order to foil various possible sophisticated attacks against the protocol. Ultimately, though, the two sides are able to exchange encrypted messages using the keys they have computed. MACs are used to check that messages are not altered in transit.

HTTPS is a secure version of HTTP, in which ordinary HTTP requests and responses are sent over a secure TLS connection. URLs for HTTPS begin with the prefix https://, and requests are sent by default to port 443 instead of port 80, which is used by ordinary HTTP.

Because the server sends its certificate to the client during the TLS set-up, its identity is verified. The certificates are validated using the publicly trusted CAs' root certificates distributed with the browser. Browsers generally display a padlock icon to indicate that an HTTPS connection has been successfully established. Clicking on the padlock shows details of the certificate, so that the identity of its owner can be checked. If the certificate is an EV certificate, a stronger indication of the reliability is given, usually by all or part of the address bar turning green.

If a server offers a certificate that is not signed by a recognized CA, or has expired, or does not match the request's domain, the browser displays a prominent warning. Most browsers advise users not to proceed at this point, although they do not actually prevent users continuing with the connection. Many respectable sites have incorrectly configured certificates, so users have become accustomed to such warnings and may ignore them.

A full description of the topics we have briefly summarized in these notes, together with sample code, can be found in the book *A Web Developer's Guide to Secure Communication* in this series.

Glossary

access control list (ACL)
A list of users associated with a *resource* and an operation, such that the users on the list are those who are authorized to perform the operation on that resource.

accessor property
In ECMAScript 5, a *property* that is defined by a pair of getter and setter methods, allowing computation to be performed while obtaining or storing the property's value.

access token
A unique value that is used as a surrogate for a user's *credentials* in calls to APIs protected by *OAuth*. An access token is issued by the API provider and must be used subsequently in calls to an API that require *authorization*.

AES (the Advanced Encryption Standard)
A complex *secret key cipher*, adopted as a US Federal Standard in 2002.

attribute
One of the named values making up a *cookie*.

authentication
In Web applications, the process of determining the identity of the user or program sending an *HTTP request*. Generally, the process of verifying the identity of a person, program or other entity.

authorization
The process of determining whether an operation requested by a particular person, program or other entity should be permitted.

authorization endpoint
A URL to which users are redirected to authenticate themselves and to agree to permit access by a specified program to an API protected by *OAuth*.

Base 64 encoding

A method of ensuring that data consists only of printable characters that can be transmitted safely over networks. Groups of three bytes (24 bits) are each treated as four 6-bit values, which are mapped to a limited character set (A–Z, a–z, 0–9, + and /), with = being used as padding if the data is not an exact multiple of three bytes in length.

bcrypt

A cryptographic hash function, based on the **Blowfish** cipher, which can be made to execute arbitrarily slowly by specifying a cost factor. Often used for hashing passwords.

block cipher

A type of *cipher* that operates on blocks of bits (often 64 or 128 bits) of *plaintext* at a time.

Blowfish

A *block cipher* comprising a *Feistel network* using 16 rounds that can take *keys* of any length between 32 and 448 bits. *Sub-keys* are generated by combining the key with random digits of the hexadecimal expansion of π. Blowfish was one of the candidate *ciphers* for replacing **DES**.

brute force attack

Any attack against a security mechanism which takes the form of an exhaustive search. In particular, an attempt to discover the contents of a *ciphertext* made simply by trying all possible *keys* until an intelligible *plaintext* emerges.

CAPTCHA

A simple puzzle, usually requiring the recognition of some distorted text, that is used to verify that a form is being filled in by a human, not a program. CAPTCHAs should be easy for humans to solve but ideally impossible for programs. The name is said to stand for "Completely Automated Public Turing test to tell Computers and Humans Apart".

certification authority (CA)
An entity that digitally signs *public key certificates* so that the certificates' authenticity can be verified.

cipher
The combination of an *encryption* algorithm and its inverse *decryption* algorithm.

ciphertext
The output of an *encryption* algorithm. Ciphertext should be unintelligible unless it is decrypted using the corresponding *decryption* algorithm and a *key* that matches the encryption key used to encrypt it.

client
See *client/server*.

client/server
The model of interaction in a distributed system such as the Internet in which a client program running on one computer sends a *request* to a server program, which listens for requests, usually on another computer, and when it receives one, sends back a *response* after performing some computation.

collision resistance
A property of good *cryptographic hash functions*, which ensures that it is infeasible to generate a pair of strings that hash to the same value.

controller
A component of an *MVC* application responsible for coordinating *views* and *models*.

cookie
In the context of the World Wide Web, a piece of information in the form of a short string of text, which can be sent as part of an *HTTP response*,

stored by a browser and included in *requests* sent to the *server* that sent the cookie. Cookies are typically used to keep track of visitors to a Web site.

credentials
The information used to identify a user or other entity for *authentication*, often consisting of a user name or email address and a password.

cross-site scripting
A type of attack against Web applications that uses JavaScript embedded in a Web page to perform malicious actions in the browsers of visitors to the page.

cryptanalysis
The science of breaking codes. In the case of *ciphers*, the analysis of *encrypted* messages to discover the *decryption key*.

cryptographic hash function
A function that generates fixed-length values from arbitrary strings. A useful cryptographic hash function will have the property that it is infeasible to determine the original string from the hash value, and will be *collision-resistant*.

cryptography
The science of *ciphers*.

decryption
The process of turning *ciphertext* back into *plaintext*.

DES (the Data Encryption Standard)
A *cipher* adopted as a US Federal Standard in 1976 for encrypting sensitive data. DES is based on a *Feistel network*, using a 56-bit *key*. It is now considered insecure and has been succeeded by *AES*.

digital signature
A *message digest* encrypted using a *key* to prevent tampering with the message's contents and provide an assurance of its origin.

domain validation certificates
The least secure class of *public key certificates* used for securing Web sites. Domain validation certificates can be obtained cheaply and the *Certification Authority* only checks that the applicant is the rightful owner of the domain named on the certificate.

EJS (Embedded JavaScript)
A templating system for embedding executable JavaScript in HTML, which may be used for defining views in *Express*.

encryption
The process of turning *plaintext* into *ciphertext*.

Express
A Web application development framework for *Node.js*.

extended validation (EV) certificates
The most secure type of *public key certificates* used for securing Web sites. EV certificates are expensive and can only be obtained after the *Certification Authority* has made extensive checks on the identity of the applicant. Most browsers display a special indication in the address bar when a connection has been successfully made to a site protected by an EV certificate.

Feistel network
An algorithm for *encrypting* blocks of data in several rounds, using a *key* and a round function. Feistel networks are often used as the basis of *block ciphers*.

foreign key
In databases using the *relational model*, a column in one table containing values that appear as *primary keys* in another table, used for representing *one-to-many relationships*.

hash value
The value computed by a *cryptographic hash function*.

HMAC
A common name for a *Keyed-Hash Message Authentication Code*.

HTTP (HyperText Transfer Protocol)
A simple protocol for the fast transmission over the Internet of hypertext information, usually documents marked up in HTML.

HTTP Basic Authentication
A challenge/response *authentication* mechanism, built in to *HTTP*, in which *credentials* are sent over the network in *plaintext* form.

HTTP Digest Authentication
A challenge/response *authentication* mechanism, built in to *HTTP*, in which *credentials* are sent over the network in encrypted form.

HTTPS
A protocol that is identical to *HTTP* except that all messages are sent over a *TLS/SSL* connection, which allows the *server's* identity to be *authenticated* and the data to be *encrypted*.

injection attack
A type of attack against Web applications, in which a *request* is specially constructed so that some of the data it contains is executed as code (especially SQL queries), or used to address protected data illicitly.

JSON (JavaScript Object Notation)
A textual format for data interchange, in which structured data is represented in the form of JavaScript objects and arrays.

key
A parameter to the *encryption* or *decryption* function of a *cipher*. In the case of encryption, the key determines the *ciphertext* produced for any *plaintext*. In the case of decryption it determines the plaintext produced from any ciphertext. Only if the key used for decryption matches the key for encryption will the decrypted plaintext be identical to the original. (Matching keys are not necessarily equal.)

keyed hash function
A *cryptographic hash function* that uses a *key*, so that the *message digest* generated by the function can only be checked by a person or program that has access to the key. This prevents tampering if the message is intercepted.

Keyed-Hash Message Authentication Code
A standard construction using a *cryptographic hash function* to generate a *MAC*.

MAC (message authentication code)
The value computed by a *keyed hash function*.

man-in-the-middle attack
A form of attack in which the attacker interposes himself between the *principals* of an exchange of messages, without being detected, so that to each of the principals he appears to be the other. This enables him to eavesdrop on and tamper with the data being exchanged.

many-to-many relationship
In databases, a relationship between two sets of entities with the property that each member of the first set may be related to more than one member of the second set, and each member of the second set may be related to

more than one member of the first set. In the **relational model**, the sets of entities are represented by tables, and the relationship by a table containing pairs of *foreign keys* from the two related tables.

masked input value
A value typed in an `input` element, usually of type `password`, in an HTML form, whose characters are concealed on the Web page by being replaced by a row of asterisks or bullets.

MD5
A well-established *cryptographic hash function*, which generates 128-bit *hash values*. MD5 is no longer considered adequately secure.

message digest
Another name for *hash value*.

model
A component of an **MVC** application that accesses and modifies data, which is usually stored in a database.

MVC (Model-View-Controller)
A software pattern often used in Web applications, in which the application is divided into three types of module, each with its own responsibilities: *models*, *views* and *controllers*.

Node-DBI
A database-agnostic driver, in the form of a *Node.js* module, which provides a single API for several different database systems.

Node.js
A system for executing JavaScript programs outside a Web browser, consisting of a high-performance interpreter and a library which makes extensive use of callbacks and events. Node.js is most often used in Web *servers*.

nonce
A value, usually a random string, which is generated to be used once only. Nonces are used to ensure that messages in secure exchanges cannot be used again.

noSQL
A loosely-defined term that includes several database systems which do not use the *relational model*, and which are suitable for distributed implementation on a large scale.

OAuth
A protocol framework that provides secure means for a Web application to authorize some other application to access protected data on behalf of a user.

Object-Relational Mapping (ORM)
A software component that allows tables in a relational database to be manipulated as if they were classes, with the rows being objects..

offline attack
An attempt to obtain users' passwords illicitly by decrypting the stored *hash values* in the password database, often by a *brute force attack*. Offline attacks require the attackers to obtain a copy of the database.

one-to-many relationship
In databases, a relationship between two sets of entities with the property that each member of the first set may be related to more than one member of the second set, but each member of the second set may be related to at most one member of the first set. In the *relational model*, the sets of entities are represented by tables, and the relationship by a column in the second table containing a *foreign key* from the first.

online attack
An attempt to obtain users' passwords illicitly by making repeated attempts to log in to their accounts using guessed passwords.

OpenId

A decentralized **authentication** protocol that allows users to log in to multiple Web sites using a single set of **credentials**.

OpenId provider

Any Web site that issues and authenticates **credentials** for use by **OpenId**.

OpenId Provider Endpoint URL

The URL provided by an **OpenId provider** for performing **authentication**. Users' browsers are redirected to this URL when they attempt to log in to a site that allows users to log in with **OpenId**.

OpenSSL

A well-established Open Source library that implements many important cryptographic algorithms, as well as providing an implementation of **TLS/SSL**. OpenSSL is written in C, but wrappers for it are available which allow it to be used from almost any programming language.

organization validation certificates

A class of **public key certificates** used for securing Web sites. Organization validation certificates provide an intermediate level of security between **domain validation certificates** and **EV certificates**. Some vetting of the person or organization applying for the certificate is performed before an organization validation certificate is issued.

packet sniffer

A program that captures some or all of the packets passing through a given network. Packet sniffers are used legitimately by system administrators for trouble-shooting and optimizing networks, but are also commonly used by attackers for eavesdropping on network traffic.

phishing

A way of trying to persuade people to disclose confidential information unwittingly to criminals. Usually, phishing is achieved by setting up a Web site that resembles the genuine site of an organization such as a bank, and then drawing users to it by sending fake email messages, often purporting to alert the victim to security breaches. When a user responds to the message and visits the fake site, they are asked for passwords, credit card details, and so on, which are then passed on to the criminals.

PKI (public key infrastructure)
The combination of file formats, organizations and procedures for using and administering *public key certificates*.

plaintext
The input to *encryption* and the output from *decryption*. Readable text which is made unintelligible by being converted to *ciphertext*.

primary key
In the *relational model* of data, a column in a table for which each row has a unique value, so that the primary key's value identifies exactly one row in the table.

principals
The participants – people, organizations, programs or devices – in an exchange of data.

property
In JavaScript, a constituent part of an object, comprising an association between a name and a value.

Provider Authentication Policy Extension
An extension to the *OpenId* specification, providing a mechanism by which *relying parties* can require an *OpenId provider* to use a specified method of *authentication*.

public key certificate
An electronic document containing a public *key*, some form of identification of the key's owner (such as their email address), and usually some other metadata. The certificate is authenticated by the digital signature of a *Certification Authority*.

public key cryptography
The theory and practice of *ciphers* in which a pair of mathematically-related but distinct *keys*, known as the public and private keys, are used for *encryption* and *decryption*, instead of the single key used for both operations in *secret key cryptography*. Public key cryptography can be used for purposes of authentication as well as encryption.

publicly trusted CAs
Certification Authorities whose root certificates are distributed with the major Web browsers.

rainbow attack
A method of discovering the *plaintext* of encrypted passwords by comparing their *hash values* with the entries in a *rainbow table* containing entries for dictionary words, names and other strings likely to be used as passwords. The pre-computed table can be used repeatedly, for example, whenever a password database is illicitly obtained by attackers.

rainbow table
A pre-computed, efficiently organized table of *hash values*, usually containing entries for common passwords and other strings likely to be used as passwords. Rainbow tables are often used in *offline attacks*.

realm
A collection of resources, usually part of a single site, protected by *HTTP Basic Authentication* or *HTTP Digest Authentication*, which can all be accessed using the same *credentials*.

reCAPTCHA
A type of *CAPTCHA* which makes use of images of words from scanned documents that have not been automatically recognized, and uses the results of successful attempts to improve the database of recognized words.

redirection endpoint
A URL, provided by a site wishing to access another that is protected by *OAuth*, which is used as the destination of redirects during the OAuth exchanges between the two sites.

relational model
A method of organizing large collections of persistent data, in which the database is organized as a collection of tables, each containing rows of data.

relying party
An application that allows *OpenId authentication*.

replay attack
The fraudulent or malicious repetition of any network transmission which legitimately authorizes a transaction only once, but is intercepted and repeated.

request
In communication protocols, a message sent from a *client* to a *server*.

request line
The first line of an *HTTP request*, specifying the operation and *resource* being requested.

reset token
A unique random string, generated when a user sends a *request* to reset a forgotten password. The reset token is sent to the user by email as part of a link and stored in the database as part of the user's record, so that the subsequent *HTTP request* to reset the password can be verified as coming from the rightful user.

resource
An entity, identified by a URL, which responds to a specific set of operations invoked by way of *HTTP requests*.

response
In communication protocols, a message sent from a *server* to a *client*.

role
A class of users who are authorized to perform a certain set of restricted operations.

root certificate
The highest level of *public key certificate* used by a *PKI*. Root certificates cannot be verified by a *digital signature*, but must be trusted.

route middleware
In *Express*, callbacks which are passed as arguments to routing methods, to be called before control is passed to the specified *controller* method. Objects containing data obtained from the *request* and to be added to the *response* are passed as arguments to route middleware.

RSA
The first practical *public key cryptography* system, invented in 1978 and named after the initials of its inventors (Rivest, Shamir and Adleman).

salting
The practice of adding a unique random string to a password before computing and storing its *hash value*. This has the effect of foiling *rainbow attacks*.

same-origin policy
A restriction imposed by Web browsers on the domains to which *cookies* are sent in *requests*. The policy stipulates that a cookie will be sent with any requests to the domain that issued it, or to any sub-domains of that domain, unless it includes a domain attribute, which may restrict or expand the set of domains to which it is sent.

secret key cryptography
The theory and practice of *ciphers* in which a single *key* is used for *encryption* and *decryption*. The key must therefore be shared between the *principals* in the exchange but kept secret from eavesdroppers.

server
See *client/server.*

session
An object or some other associative data structure, which appears to persist between *requests* from the same source.

SHA (Secure Hash Algorithm)
A family of *cryptographic hash functions*, comprising SHA-1, which produces 160-bit *hash values*, and the more secure SHA-2 family, a set of functions which generate hash values of various lengths. The individual SHA-2 algorithms (SHA-224, SHA-256, SHA-384 and SHA-512) are identified by the length of the hash value.

shared key cryptography
An alternative name for *secret-key cryptography.*

shared secret
A value, such as a password, known only to the *principals* of an exchange, which is used to authenticate their identities or to encrypt messages.

single sign-in service
Any service, such as *OpenId*, which allows users to log in to multiple Web sites using a single set of *credentials*.

singular resource
A *resource* that is not part of a set of resources, and so can be accessed using URLs that do not include an identifier for a specific object.

SQL injection
A type of *injection attack*, in which malicious SQL queries are embedded in *request* data.

SSL (Secure Sockets Layer)
The precursor of TLS, now incorporated in *TLS/SSL*.

symmetrical cipher
A *cipher* based on *secret key cryptography*.

TLS/SSL (Transport Layer Security/Secure Sockets Layer)
A secure protocol used on the Internet for the exchange of data packets. TLS/SSL is used to transport messages belonging to higher-level protocols in a secure manner. TLS is the standard version of the protocol, but it is often referred to by the initials of its predecessor, *SSL*.

triple DES (3DES)
A more secure variant of *DES*, in which the *ciphertext* is generated from the *plaintext* by successively encrypting, decrypting and then encrypting again, using DES and three distinct *keys*.

view
A component of an *MVC* application responsible for presenting data to users, usually by inserting values from a *model* into a template.

X.509
The *PKI* presently used on the Web.

XRDS
An XML-based language used as the format of the *response* to a *Yadis request* to find an *OpenId Provider Endpoint URL*.

Yadis
A discovery protocol used by *OpenId* to find *OpenId Provider Endpoint URLs*.

Index

Page references in **bold italics**
indicate glossary definitions.

Lightning Source UK Ltd.
Milton Keynes UK
UKOW030439111012

200381UK00001B/7/P